K. Koblik

K. Koblik

THE ILLUSTRATED GUIDE TO
CELTIC
MYTHOLOGY

THE ILLUSTRATED GUIDE TO
CELTIC MYTHOLOGY

T.W. ROLLESTON

Introduction by Arthur Cotterell

CRESCENT BOOKS
NEW YORK • AVENEL

Sheet bronze cauldron (half-title page) found in the River Thames (British Museum).

Connemara (frontispiece), evening view of lough and hills near Maam Cross. Part of the ancient kingdom of Connacht on the Atlantic coast, which was the last part of Celtic Ireland to be conquered by the English.

Shield and sword (above) from the Thames at Battersea, London. The beautifully decorated shield was probably made for ceremonial use. (Illustration from Kemble, Franks and Latham, *Horae Ferales*, 1863.)

This 1995 edition published by Crescent Books, distributed by Random House Value Publishing, Inc. 40 Engelhard Avenue, Avenel, New Jersey 07001.

Random House
New York • Toronto • London • Sydney • Auckland

Copyright this edition © Studio Editions Ltd 1993

ISBN 0-517-12179-4

Printed and bound in Singapore

10, 9, 8, 7, 6, 5, 4, 3, 2, 1

CONTENTS

INTRODUCTION

Because the overwhelming majority of the myths retold in this volume are of Irish origin, the cursory reader might well conclude that the home of Celtic mythology is indeed the emerald isle. In one respect alone would such a judgment be correct. The Irish have always esteemed the *filidh*, "the poet", with the result that even after their conversion to Christianity in the fifth century great trouble was taken to write down the ancient sagas. The oldest of these texts were the works of monks. It may seem strange that the first Christian communities should have devoted such energy to preserving a pagan litera-ture, but there is some evidence to suggest that St. Patrick's defeat of the old Celtic religion was so complete that the recitation of the sagas could continue to delight noble auditors without any jeopardy to their souls. Quite possibly the clear division of roles in pre-Christian times between the poet and the priest (*drui*) also helped. The Irish bard was able to go on reciting poems about the deeds of pagan gods and heroes because they were already seen as enter-tainment. Something of their original potency seems to have survived, how-ever. Irish legend insists that the Devil was absolutely incapable of entering a dwelling where the exploits of a hero were being sung.

The first home of the Celts was middle Europe, in particular the region between the Rhine and the Danube. From the fifth century B.C. these fierce tribesmen expanded their control over large parts of the Continent, and one band even reached Asia Minor. In 278 B.C. it crossed the Hellespont and embarked on a campaign of destruction: its tactics comprised surprise attacks and fast movement and staying nowhere for long. At last these Celts carved out a kingdom for themselves, which was known as Galatia. Other bands had by then settled in Spain, France, northern Italy, Austria, Hungary and the Balkans. One of them sacked Rome in 385 B.C., but the Romans slowly re-covered their strength and conquered nearly all the lands which the Celts had populated. They remained independent in only the outlying parts of the British Isles. Except in unoccupied Ireland, Romanization led to the decline of Celtic religion. That it survived intact for so much longer there is undoubtedly one reason for the richness of Irish mythology. How typical the surviving Irish sagas were it is now impossible to tell. Apart from the stories contained in the

The Chief Druid was sometimes portrayed as a humble natural philosopher, holding a branch of oak, a tree regarded as sacred by the Celts. (Illustration from Rowlands, *Mona Antiqua Restaura*, 1723.)

Beginning of St Mark's Gospel (opposite), detail from the Book of Kells (Trinity College, Dublin). As well as recording pagan tales, Christian monks of the British Isles used complex early Celtic decoration for their ornamented manuscripts.

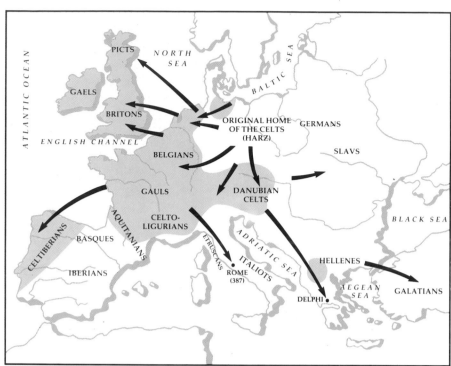

The Movement of the Celts after the Hallstatt Period took them to most parts of Europe, where they became known under different names, such as Gauls, Britons and so on, according to the languages they spoke.

Bronze mask from South Cadbury, Somerset, height 13.3 cm, mid-first century A.D. The Celtic cult of the severed head was reflected in stone statues of heads and metal masks of all sizes.

Welsh *Mabinogi*, a collection of which the earliest manuscripts date from the fourteenth century, there is nothing else to use as a comparison.

The Celts relied on the oral transmission of their religious beliefs, and so modern commentators are obliged to turn to the historical records of their Roman conquerors for assistance. The use of such testimony is not without its dangers, if only because the ten-year struggle for control of Gaul left a vivid impression on the Roman consciousness. A frustrated warlord like Julius Caesar was at pains to stress the barbarity of his opponents, in part to justify the one million slaves his own army took as booty during a hard-fought series of campaigns. Thus the blood-thirsty sacrifices of the Gauls (as the Celts living in France were called) were carefully contrasted with the civilized behaviour of the legions. According to Caesar, the Gauls were "extremely superstitious. Consequently, people suffering from serious illnesses, and people involved in the dangers of battle, make, or promise to make, human sacrifice; the druids officiate at these sacrifices. For they believe that the only way of preserving one man's life is to let another die in his place. Regular tribal sacrifices are held, at which colossal figures made of wickerwork are filled with living men, and then set alight so that the victims burn to death. The Gauls believe that the gods prefer it if the people sacrificed are convicted criminals, but whenever there is a shortage of such victims, they even go to the extent of burning innocent men."

Such descriptions of Celtic sacrifice were later embellished by other classical authors. Strabo relates how the Gauls "beat victims to death with arrows or impaled them in temples; or, after constructing a giant of wood and straw, they pushed in livestock, wild animals of all kinds, and human beings and offered the whole lot in a holocaust". And the close companion of Nero, the poet Lucan, speaks of "those who appease with detestable blood the ferocious Teutates, the hideous Esus at his cruel hearth, and Taranis at altars no less inhuman than that of the Scythian Diana". Here, three of the greatest gods of the Continental Celts are linked with bloodthirsty rites of worship. Whatever view we decide to take of these reports, there is no doubt about the cult of the severed head amongst the Celts. Like many warriors, they removed the heads of enemies slain in battle and attached them to the necks of their horses, or to the sides of their chariots. Some of these trophies were embalmed in cedar oil and carefully preserved as evidence of victory on the battlefield. Others were embedded in cavities hollowed out of doorposts and lintels. In the Irish sagas much is made of the skill of heroes in taking heads. Cuchulain, returning to Emain Macha after his first battle, is described as having three heads on his chariot and "nine heads in one hand and ten in the other, and these he brandished at the warriors in token of his valour and prowess".

Conall Cearnach, "of the Victories", was the foster-brother of the Ulster hero Cuchulain, and his avenger when he slew Lewy on the banks of the Liffey. The head and hand of Cuchulain had been carried off and buried by Lewy under a

Hadrian's Wall was built across North England from the Solway Firth to the mouth of the Tyne around 120 A.D. as a defence for the Roman invaders.

View of the Lakes of Killarney, Munster. The mild climate, subtropical vegetation and rare birds of south-west Ireland have given rise to countless legends connected with local sites.

mound at Tara, the residence of the High Kings of Ireland. On another occasion Conall of the Victories even managed to succour a severed head belonging to the High King Conaire Mór. It happened that Conaire Mór and his followers were surprised on the way back home to Tara. During the close-fought encounter, the High King was overcome with thirst and Conall volunteered to go for water. When the Ulsterman returned, the fight was over and Conaire Mór's head had been cut off. Conall gave the severed head a drink whereupon it spoke and thanked him.

The exploits of Conall and Cuchulain are celebrated in the Red Branch cycle of sagas, the Irish equivalent of the *Iliad*. Also known as the Ulster cycle, its tales are chiefly connected with the *Táin Bó Cuailgne*, the "Cattle-raid of Cuailgne". The object of this invasion was a famous brown bull which was kept in Cuailgne (or Cooley), a district of Ulster. Queen Maev of Connacht persuaded her husband, Ailell, to invade Ulster in order to add the beast to her own herd. During the invasion a strange debility prevented the Ulster warriors from offering any effective resistance. It was caused by a curse laid on the kingdom by Macha, a goddess of war. In Emain Macha, the seat of the Ulster king, the greatest champions were confined to their beds, so that "there was no hand that could lift a spear." Only the youthful Cuchulain was able to carry on a defence: single-handed he delayed the army of Connacht, until the curse no longer undermined the strength of Ulster's warriors. On one occasion he slew the enemy scouts sent ahead in two chariots, and impaled their severed heads on the four prongs of a forked pole he had cut from a nearby wood. No one dared to advance beyond this gruesome marker until a Connacht hero succeeded in pulling out "the pole as it was driven in, with the fingers of one hand". Seventeen chariots were broken in the effort necessary to uproot the pole. By such devices, as well as lightning attacks on stragglers, Cuchulain slowed the advance of the Connacht host, although he could not alone prevent the eventual capture of the brown bull by Queen Maev's forces.

The kingdom of Ulster was saved through the sacrifice of Sualtam Mac Roth, Cuchulain's mortal father. His real one was none other than the sun god Lugh. Unable to raise the men of Ulster to action, Sualtam wheeled round his horse so angrily that the sharp rim of his shield sliced off his own head. Yet the cry to arms still issued from its mouth, and the Ulster king had it placed on a pillar. At last the message "began to penetrate, and the glazed eyes of the warriors began to glow, and slowly the spell of Macha's curse was lifted from their minds and bodies".

A plundering expedition, usually a cattle-raid (*táin*), occupies a central place in many sagas. Another event favoured by the Irish bard is a journey, often a fabulous voyage. Such an adventure befell Maeldun, a lord of the Aran Isles, when he learned of his true descent and the murder of his father. Going in search of the killers, Maeldun sailed for nearly four years among strange islands inhabited by giant ants, talking birds, monstrous dogs, demon horses, fire-like creatures, magic sheep, black weepers, intoxicating fruit, laughing folk, powerful smiths, and hermits. On one particular island, he bathed in a sacred lake and renewed his youth. When he finally found the men he sought, close to his own home, Maeldun agreed to make peace in gratitude for a safe return to Ireland. This ancient story was undoubtedly the inspiration for the Christian epic *The Voyage of Brendan*, one of the most popular tales of the Middle Ages. A similar story may have suggested to Jonathan Swift the idea for *Gulliver's Travels*. Though Swift knew no Irish, he had literary friends who were capable of translating into English the journey of Iubdan, the ruler of the Wee Folk, to the Ulster king Fergus Mac Leda.

Besides the Ulster cycle, three other groups of sagas have been identified. They are the Mythological cycle, the Fenian or Ossianic cycle, and the cycle of the Kings. The first one relates the various invasions of Ireland from Noah's granddaughter Cesair to the sons of Milesius, a Scythian warrior from Spain. Most of the myths, however, are concerned with the action of the Tuatha De Danann, "the people of the goddess Dana". Under their leader Nuada, the

The Death of Cuchulain, bronze statue by Oliver Sheppard, in the Dublin General Post Office. Erected after the 1916 Easter Uprising, this memorial symbolizes those who fought for Irish independence.

Lyons (shown here in a French engraving of the sixteenth century) is one of many European cities which owe their names to the ancient Celtic god Lugh. Others include Laon and Leiden.

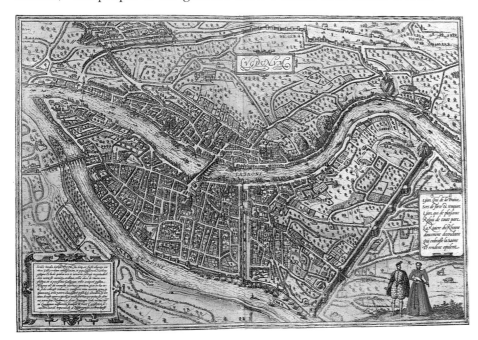

Danaans came through the air to Ireland from a northern country and landed on a mountain in Connacht. In their first battle with the Firbolg, then the dominant people, Nuada lost his hand and had to relinquish his leadership as a consequence. At first he wore an artificial hand on the stump; hence his name Nuada Argetlámh, "of the Silver Hand". Later his own hand grew so that he could become king again. His followers were believed to be the ancestors of all Irish scholars, for the Danaans were well versed in the arts, masters of sorcery and marvels, and great magicians. It is not unlikely that once they were objects of a cult. Their greatest artist was the sun god Lugh, who joined Nuada at Tara, originally as a carpenter. But Lugh soon showed himself accomplished in every field. When he played the harp, the god had the power to put his audience to sleep, make it weep, or smile with joy. One of the chief Irish deities, Lugh was the counterpart of the Welsh Lleu Llaw Gyffes, Lleu "of the Ready Hand". On the Continent he would appear to relate to Lugoves, whose name is commemorated in place names such as Laon, Leiden and Lyon. This champion of contests instituted horse racing, ball games and other meetings. Presumably these were held at Lugavalium, Roman Carlisle.

Echoes of the Irish sagas are indeed found in the Welsh *Mabinogi*. But this tiny collection of Welsh myths turns almost exclusively on sovereignty. The stories deal with challenges to royal authority, often from a supernatural source. Thus Pwyll, a ruler of Dyfed, offended the king of the underworld and had to placate Arawn by changing places with him for a year. As Arawn was being harried by a rival, Havgan, it was understood that Pwyll would have to meet this awesome warrior in single combat. During the period that he impersonated Arawn, Pwyll was instructed to learn the manners of his court, which was renowned for its courtesy and propriety. He enjoyed the company and conversation of Arawn's queen, the most charming woman he had ever met, and at night chastely shared her bed. Having defeated Havgan and reunited the underworld kingdom, Pwyll returned to Dyfed where he discovered universal praise for the excellence of Arawn's rule. After an exchange of gifts, Pwyll adopted the title of Pen Annwn, "Lord of the Underworld", and resumed the Dyfed throne as a model king.

However, another challenge in the form of Rhiannon caused him temporary grief. She appeared near a magic mound "in garments that shone like gold, and sitting on a pure white horse". He sent men to greet her, but no one could catch her up. Only on Pwyll's own declaration of love would Rhiannon deign to stop. They were duly married and a son was born, named Gwri. But one of Rhiannon's rejected suitors stole the child in revenge. The women charged with Gwri's safety were so afraid of the king's anger that they framed Rhiannon. Blamed for devouring her own child, she was condemned to sit by the gate of Pwyll's stronghold and tell strangers of her crime, then offer to carry them on her back into his hall. During the period of Rhiannon's penance, the missing boy was fostered by a distant chieftain who had found him one night in his stable. Finally Gwri was brought to Pwyll and the truth revealed: Rhiannon was reinstated as queen and her son renamed Pryderi, "Worry".

Rhiannon and her son are clearly associated with horses. Even her punishment is to act like a beast of burden. This association has led to the suggestion that she was none other than the Celtic horse goddess Epona, known from Roman inscriptions. The widespread diffusion of her cult is well attested. In Rome an image of Epona adorned the entrance to the stables of the imperial

The Adventures of Pwyll (illustration by Dorothea Braby), is typical of many Celtic tales in its combination of human and otherworld characters.

guard. She was portrayed mounted and unmounted, with a child or a foal at her side. This mingling of worship under the Romans was in part a consequence of the conquest of the lands surrounding the Mediterranean Sea. While none could resist the tramp of the legions, the conquered peoples discovered to their surprise that the citizens of Rome were almost defenceless against foreign religions. Although particularly true of the relationship between Greece and Rome, the process of assimilation also encompassed several Celtic deities. Out of such an amalgam of beliefs may have derived the legendary cycle of valorous deeds of Knights of the Round Table.

There are allusions to a ruler like Arthur in two old Welsh poems, dating from the early seventh century. Two centuries later the monk Nennius, in his *History of Britain*, states that Arthur was a leader of troops defending the country against foreign invaders. Following the withdrawal of the Roman

Glastonbury Abbey, Somerset. The tombs of Arthur and Guinevere were said to have been discovered here in around 1190 under a stone inscription which identified Glastonbury with Avalon.

Arthur and the Knights of the Breton cycle (north-facing portal of Modena Cathedral, North Italy). The stories of British Arthur were retold all over Europe throughout the Middle Ages.

Poster for Excalibur. John Boorman's 1981 film adaptation of Malory's *Morte d'Arthur* tells the story of Arthur from his birth to his final battle.

legions from Britain around 410, the hard-pressed inhabitants would have cherished the idea of an undying saviour, especially as they were being over-run by the Angles, Saxons and Jutes. That Arthur remained a focus for Cornish and Welsh political aspirations there can be little doubt. The inscription on his tomb at Glastonbury catches the flavour of his legendary life and undeath. It reads: "Here lies Arthur, king that was, king that shall be." As late as 1113 the denial of his undeath, by the servants of French visitors to the Cornish town of Bodmin, provoked a riot. In his mysterious departure for Avalon, after the slaying of nearly all his followers, Arthur enacted a typical Celtic myth of the sleeping hero. One version of Finn Mac Cumhal's end says that the great Irish warrior is not dead but is spell-bound in a cave, waiting for the call to help his country in its hour of need. The leader of the Fianna, a band of dedicated fight-ers of austere habits, Finn Mac Cumhal is celebrated in the Fenian or Ossianic cycle of Irish sagas.

Impetus to the Arthurian legend was given by the publication of Geoffrey of Monmouth's *History of the British Kingdom* in 1137. This chronicle and its adaption in French verse by Wace some twenty years afterwards were already part of a cycle of stories about a marvellous king and his fearless knights, who wholeheartedly accepted a challenge and never hesitated to rescue a woman in distress. For three centuries the rise and fall of the Round Table comprised the great medieval myth, but Christianized though it was by successive authors, the Celtic origin of the tales could never be entirely disguised. Besides the magical sword Excalibur, which Arthur alone could draw from the stone, there was that enigmatic utensil, the Holy Grail. A cup from the Last Supper, it was used by Joseph of Arimathea to gather some blood from Jesus' pierced side at the Crucifixion. Later he brought the Holy Grail to England, where it was lost. The search for this mysterious cup preoccupied the Knights of the Round Table, although only Galahad, Lancelot's son, was allowed to approach the Holy Grail and ascend to heaven. The Church was always uneasy about its closeness to the Celtic cauldron, which provided abundance and restored people to life. Arawn possessed one. Then again, there was the difficulty of explaining the guardian of the Holy Grail, the so-called Fisher King, who lay wounded and immobile, neither dead nor living.

Excalibur (opposite), Arthur's magical sword, has inspired many interpretations of the old stories. In this illustration from the medieval *Roman de Lancelot*, Arthur has instructed Bedivere to return Excalibur to the lake.

vant gifles voit que
faire li couient. sire
uient arriere la ou les
pee estoit si la prent et la retorne
ce aregarder et aplaindre mlt
durement et dist tot en plorant.

CHAPTER I

THE HISTORY AND CULTURE OF THE CELTS

T he true Celts, if we accept the opinion of the ancient historians of Greece and Rome, were a tall, fair, warlike race, whose place of origin was somewhere around the sources of the Danube and who spread their dominion by conquest and by peaceful infiltration over Mid-Europe, Gaul, Spain and the British Isles. No contemporary chronicles of their own have come down to us, yet from their ornaments, coins and weapons, and from the names which often cling in altered forms to the places where they lived, much can be deduced.

The term Celt is first found in the Greek historian Hecataeus in about 500 B.C. Archaeological research, however, suggests that the Celts may well have emerged from central Europe as a distinctive group some time before that. Excavations at Hallstatt in Austria have revealed the existence of a flourishing early Celtic civilization there around 700 B.C. Over the following five hundred years or so the Celtic peoples expanded their sphere of influence over much of Continental Europe and the British Isles. By the end of the first century A.D., however, the Germanic tribes were pressing into north-western Europe and most of the Mediterranean region, Gaul and Britain had fallen under the yoke of Rome. Celtic populations were driven back into the more remote areas on the western fringes: Brittany, Cornwall, Devon, Wales, south-west Scotland and north-west England.

Although there are no remaining independent Celtic countries today, the Celtic language has survived in France, Ireland and Britain in the form of Breton, Irish, Welsh, Scots Gaelic and Manx. Irish, Gaelic and Manx are the closest to the early language, retaining as they do a Q sound in such words *cen* (head), where the Welsh and Breton *pen* (also head) uses a P.

According to the Roman traveller Strabo, who died in 24 A.D., the Celts were a warlike, passionate people with a love of display. Indeed, Celtic art is remarkable for its sweeping curves and undulations which are used to form complex decorations for weapons, horse trappings, collars, bracelets and brooches, and all kinds of household appliances. Other ancient historians

A Maaeata and Caledonian, Celts from Northern Britain, tattooed their bodies and often went into battle naked according to the Roman historian Isidorus. (Illustration from C. Hamilton Smith, *Ancient Costumes of Great Britain and Ireland,* 1814.)

Graves at Hallstatt, near Salzburg (opposite). In 1846 Austrian archaeologist George Ramsauer discovered almost a thousand graves of early Celts in a vast burial site by a salt mine. (Drawing by Isidor Engl.)

NORTH SEA

SCOTS

PICTS

Dumbarton

KINGDOM OF STRATHCLYDE

ANTONINE WALL

HADRIAN'S WALL

DARINI

PICTS

BRIGANTES

DOMNONII

Ulster

Connaught   Meath

Man

Eboracum
(York) ●

CAUCI

GAELS

Mona

Leinster

Gwynedd

● Deva
(Chester)

CORITANI

Lindum

GANGANI

MENAPII

ORDOVICES

Munster

Powys   CORNOVII

ICENI

IVERNI

Venta Icenorum

DOBUNI

TRINOBANTES

BRIGANTES

Dyvet   SILURES

Caerlion

● Glevum
(Gloucester)

CATUVELLAUNI

Londinium

Camulodunum
(Colchester)

ATREBATES

DUROTRIGES

CANTII

DOMNONII

REGNII

Vectis

IRISH SEA

ENGLISH CHANNEL

Map of the British Isles in Roman times,
showing the kingdoms of Ireland and
Wales, the homes of the Celtic tribes and
the chief Roman cities.

remarked on the Celtic habit of tattooing the body and artificially highlighting fair hair by washing it in lime-water. But, again according to Strabo, this fondness for personal decoration was mixed with a barbarism evident in the way warriors would ride home from battle with the heads of their fallen enemies dangling from their horses' necks. What Strabo failed to understand was the symbolic significance of the human head for Celtic peoples. They regarded it as the ultimate source of spiritual power, so that to carry off the head of a defeated enemy was to harness his sacred energy. Some even decorated skulls with gold and used them as drinking vessels.

The Celts' methods of warfare, using large hacking swords, spears thrown from fast-moving light chariots, and shrieking naked riders to instil an initial terror into their enemies, were extremely effective. Celtic warriors were well-served by a flourishing metal-working industry. Swords, spears, helmets, shields, war trumpets and chariots were all ornamented, sometimes with enamelling, which was a technique supposedly invented by the Celts. This skill was also employed to make a wide variety of iron-based tools. Iron ploughshares made it possible for them to cultivate heavy soils for which wooden implements were unsuitable, and on which they grew wheat and millet. Metal wood-working tools made their carpentry skills more sophisticated and they constructed most of their buildings from wood.

Houses were made from arched timbers with walls of wickerwork and thatched roofs. Forts, walled towns or large villages, and strongholds of the various tribes were conspicuous on many hills, while the plains were dotted by scores of open hamlets. Roads ran from town to town and barges laden with merchandise floated along the rivers. Every tribe had its coinage, and there was a thriving trade with other parts of the world in such commodities as Baltic amber and Phoenician glass.

At the basis of Celtic society was the extended family or clan. Several families made up a tribe, which operated according to its own social hierarchy from the chief down to slaves. A curious custom which is mentioned in several myths and legends was the practice of fosterage, by which the responsibility for bringing up and educating a child was taken over by another mother and father. In many cases the foster-father was the brother of the child's natural mother and the strength of the emotional and moral ties between the child and his foster-family lasted throughout the rest of his life.

Generally speaking, land was communally owned and wealth was related to the size of cattle herds. Compared to many other civilizations of the same period, women enjoyed considerable power in Celtic societies. Girls had a theoretical right to choose their own husbands; wives retained ownership of any property they brought into the marriage; and the presence in history and myth of such women as Boudicca and Maev points to the existence of formidable female warrior queens.

Although they spoke variants of the same language and shared a common name, the Celtic peoples had little sense of a common nationhood and were organized into tribal groupings, which were often at war with one another.

Iona in the sixth century. Before becoming a centre of Celtic Christianity, Iona was known as the Island of the Druids. Rounded roofs were used for both thatched and stone buildings.

Horse trappings of cast bronze, with enamel inset in the *champlevé* technique, demonstrate the technical sophistication achieved by Celtic craftsmen. (Illustration from Kemble, Franks and Latham, *Horae Ferales*, 1863.)

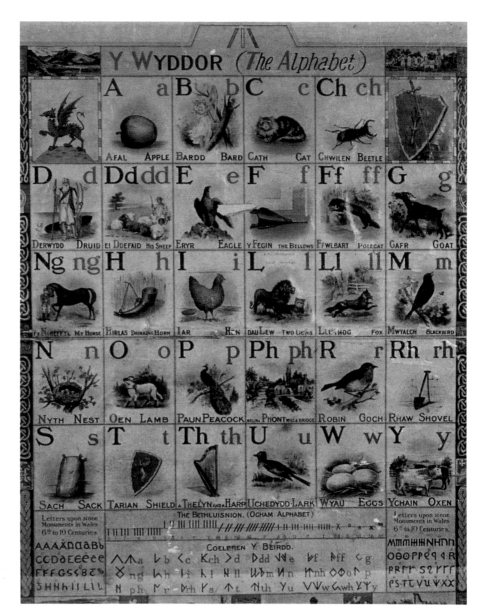

The Ogham Alphabet was included in a wallchart designed by two Welsh teachers during the nineteenth-century Celtic Revival, a movement to promote interest in ancient literature. (Welsh Folk Museum, Cardiff.)

Clonmacnois, beside the River Shannon, was an important centre of Celtic Christianity and the burial place of many Irish kings, but its position made it vulnerable to Viking attack.

Within the tribes, the king was usually elected and acted as a military leader. Warriors, intellectuals and craftsmen formed an elite beneath the king, and their importance is reflected in the roles they played in Celtic myth.

For the most part, early myths and legends were handed down orally, and responsibility for preserving the existing tradition intact and for inventing new stories and verses lay with the bards and poets. This is not to say that no means of recording existed. In Ireland the technique known as Ogham (after Ogma, who was supposed to have invented it) was probably introduced in the fourth century A.D. and spread to some other Celtic areas in west and north Britain in succeeding years. The Ogham alphabet consisted of twenty basic letters depicted by the use of vertical, horizontal and oblique strokes. Originally used on stone and wood, Ogham was eventually superseded by the more practical Roman alphabet but survives on hundreds of stone monuments, particularly in Ireland.

It is hard to disentangle any common core of early Celtic religion from the Greek and Roman religions with which it later became intermingled. The myths suggest that many of the Celtic gods and goddesses represented various aspects of nature and that they were worshipped in sacred groves. Among those who appear in most of the areas under Celtic influence were Epona the horse goddess, Lugh the sun god and Cernunnos the horned god. It is possible, however, that these were the gods of the aristocracy only, and that the common people worshipped far more localized deities who represented a particular geographical feature. Inscriptions and sculptures bear testimony to the existence of a host of minor gods, and although many are rude copies of the Roman style of religious art, some are much wilder and stranger figures—gods with triple faces and ram-headed serpents.

Seasonal festivals were held at Imbolc on 1 February, associated with the sacred flame that encouraged the sun from its winter sleep; at Beltane on 1 May, a fertility gathering with dancing round fires; at Lugnasadh on 1 August, devoted to the sun god Lugh; and at Samhain on 1 November, which was the beginning of the Celtic new year and when there was free access between this and the Otherworld. While the origins of Celtic culture and belief lie in the centuries well before the coming of Christianity, the Celtic myths and legends now available to us were not written down until long after the arrival of the Christian Church in Britain and Ireland and were undoubtedly subject to Christian influence. Many of the old deities were transformed into fairies, their supernatural powers into magic, and the great festivals were incorporated into the Christian calendar.

Although they are usually regarded as priests, the Druids were really the sovereign power among the Celtic peoples. All affairs, public and private, were subject to their authority, and they acted both as official arbitrators in local disputes and as ambassadors in wartime. Their decisions were taken as law. Indeed, the king was not allowed to speak until the Druid had done so.

As well as enjoying considerable secular power, the Druids were also responsible for ritual and religion. Trained over several years in special colleges, they were expected to study philosophy, law, verse composition and the recitation of tales. In order to preserve their mystery, the Druidic doctrines were never written down but had to be learned by rote. Like shamans of all cultures Druids were credited with the ability to foretell the future and interpret omens, to heal the sick, to impose magic prohibitions and obligations, and to gain access to the Otherworld.

The modern imagination tends to associate the Druids with megalithic monuments such as Stonehenge, but archaeological evidence has shown that these places were built by a far earlier civilization. It is likely, however, that the Druids understood their astronomical significance and were able to use them to predict eclipses and so forth. Most of the structures erected by the pre-Christian Celts themselves were made of wood and were intended for domestic or military use.

The purpose of the other stone monuments left by the megalithic culture were sometimes misinterpreted by the Celts, who nevertheless incorporated them into their own myths and beliefs. The great chambered tumulus of New Grange in Ireland, for example, was regarded on the one hand as the home of the ancient gods and on the other as the traditional burial place of the high kings. The holed stones found at the entrances to prehistoric tombs were symbols of the birth passage in rituals of initiation and rebirth, for the Druids are believed to have taught that the soul did not die with the body but passed into another body. The standing stones at Carnac in France were believed to be the place where the heroes rested on their journey to the Isles of the Blessed.

Stone figure from Boa Island, Co. Fermanagh. Dating from around the seventh century, this unnamed Celtic deity is backed by an identical figure facing in the opposite direction.

Beltany stone circle at Raphoe, Co. Donegal. Although built by ancient megalithic peoples, such monuments were regarded as sacred places by the Celts of later centuries.

CHAPTER II

THE IRISH
INVASION MYTHS

T here is nothing in the most ancient legendary literature of the Irish Gaels, which is the oldest Celtic literature in existence, no myth corresponding to the Babylonian conquest of Chaos, or the wild Norse myth of the making of Midgard out of the corpse of Ymir, or the Egyptian creation of the universe out of the primeval Water by Thoth, the Word of God. That the Druids had some doctrine on this subject it is impossible to doubt. But by resolutely confining it to the initiated and forbidding all lay speculation on the subject, they seem to have completely stifled the myth-making instinct in regard to questions of cosmogony among the people at large, and ensured that when their own order perished, their teaching, whatever it was, should die with them.

In the early Irish accounts, therefore, of the beginnings of things, it is not with the World that the narrators make their start—it is simply with their own country, with Ireland. It was the practice, indeed, to prefix to these narratives of early invasions and colonizations the Scriptural account of the making of the world and man; but what took the place of the Biblical narrative in pre-Christian days we do not know.

The Giants Causeway, Co. Antrim, was supposedly built by the giant Finn to provide stepping-stones to Scotland. Irish myth abounds in similar legendary explanations for geographical features.

Fairy palaces (opposite). The impressive passage-grave at New Grange, a few miles from Tara in Co. Meath, was said to be the home of Angus mac Og, god of love and beauty.

THE CYCLES OF IRISH LEGEND

Irish mythical and legendary literature, as we have it in the most ancient form, may be said to fall into four main divisions. They are, in chronological order, the Mythological Cycle or Cycle of the Invasions, the Ultonian or Conorian Cycle, the Ossianic or Fenian Cycle. In addition there is a great multitude of miscellaneous tales and legends which it is hard to fit into any historical framework. The Mythological Cycle, which forms the subject of this chapter, comprises the following sections: 1. The coming of Partholan into Ireland; 2. The coming of Nemed into Ireland; 3. The coming of the Firbolgs into Ireland; 4. The invasion of the *Tuatha De Dannan*, or People of the god Dana; 5. The invasion of the Milesians (Sons of Miled) from Spain, and their conquest of the People of Dana.

With the Milesians we begin to come into something resembling history—they represent, in Irish legend, the Celtic race; and from them the later ruling families of Ireland are supposed to be descended. Apart from the mythological material, the only written evidence from which early Irish history can be reconstructed is the *Leabhar Gabala* or Book of Invasions. This scholarly compilation of oral tradition, annals and genealogies was made in the ninth and twelfth centuries by monks. If the Sons of Miled can be identified with the Gaels, then the People of Dana are evidently gods and are credited with bringing the finer points of civilization to the land. The pre-Danaan settlers or invaders are huge phantom-like figures, which loom vaguely through the mists of tradition, and have little definite characterization.

THE COMING OF PARTHOLAN

The Celts believed themselves to be descended from the God of the Underworld, the God of the Dead. Partholan is said to have come into Ireland from the West, where beyond the Atlantic Ocean the Irish Fairyland, the Land of the Living was placed. There were then but three lakes in Ireland, nine rivers, and only one plain. Others were added gradually during the reign of the Partholanians. One, Lake Rury, was said to have burst out as a grave was being dug for Rury, son of Partholan.

The Partholanians, it is said, had to do battle with a strange race, called the Fomorians. They were a cruel people, representing the powers of evil. With a host of these demons Partholan fought for the lordship of Ireland, and drove them out to the northern seas, from whence they occasionally harried the country under its later rulers.

The end of the race of Partholan was that they were afflicted by pestilence, and having gathered together on the Old Plain (Senmag) for convenience of burying their dead, they all perished there, and Ireland once more lay empty for reoccupation.

This tale was told in "The Legend of Tuan mac Carell." St. Finnen, an Irish abbot of the sixth century, is said to have gone to seek hospitality from a chief named Tuan mac Carell, who dwelt not far from Finnen's monastery at Moville, Co. Donegal. Good relations were established between them, and the saint returned to his monks.

Tuan came shortly afterwards to return the visit of the saint, and invited him and his disciples to his fortress. They asked him of his name and lineage. "I am a man of Ulster," he said. "My name is Tuan, son of Carell. But once I was called Tuan, son of Starn, son of Sera, and my father, Starn, was the brother of Partholan."

"Tell us the history of Ireland," then said Finnen, and Tuan began. "After the great pestilence he alone survived in the land, and he wandered about for twenty-two years, dwelling in waste places, till at last he fell into extreme decrepitude and old age.

"Then Nemed, son of Agnoman, took possession of Ireland. He [Agnoman] was my father's brother. I saw him from the cliffs, and kept avoiding him. I was long-haired, decrepit, naked. Then one evening I fell asleep, and when I woke on the morrow I was changed into a stag. I was young again and glad of heart."

St. Finnen and the Pagan Chief. "Good relations were established between them." (Illustration from T. W. H. Rolleston, *Myths of the Celtic Race*, 1911.)

The Glens of Antrim, Northern Ireland, cut through the hills in a series of nine valleys leading down to the sea. From this part of the coast it is possible to see across the North Channel to Scotland.

Sea Eagle by Joseph Wolf. "He became a great eagle of the sea, and once more rejoiced in renewed youth."

Tuan was then king of all the deer of Ireland, and so remained all the days of Nemed and his race.

He told how the Nemedians sailed for Ireland in a fleet of thirty-two barks. They went astray on the seas for a year and a half, and most of them perished of hunger and thirst or of shipwreck. Only nine escaped—Nemed himself, with four men and four women. These landed in Ireland, and increased their numbers in the course of time till they were 8060 men and women. Then all of them mysteriously died.

Again, old age fell upon Tuan, but another transformation awaited him. "Once I was standing at the mouth of my cave and I knew that my body changed into another form. I was a wild boar. Then I became young again, and I was glad. I was king of the boar-herds in Ireland, and I returned into the lands of Ulster at the time old age and wretchedness came upon me. For it was always there that my transformations took place."

Tuan then went on to tell how Semion, son of Stariat, settled in Ireland, from whom descended the Firbolgs. Again old age came on, his strength failed him, and he underwent another transformation: he became a great eagle of the sea, and once more rejoiced in renewed youth. He then told how the People of Dana came in. After these came the Sons of Miled, who conquered the People of Dana. All this time Tuan kept the shape of the sea-eagle, till one day he was

Tuan as a salmon. "At last he was captured and brought to the wife of Carell, chief of the country." (Illustration by Arthur Rackham from James Stephens, *Irish Fairy Tales*, 1920.)

Smith god. Bronze figure of a Celtic deity from Sunderland, second to third centuries A.D. (Museum of Antiquities, Newcastle-upon-Tyne).

changed into a salmon. He rejoiced in his new life, till at last he was captured and brought to the wife of Carell, chief of the country. "The woman desired me and ate me by herself, whole, so that I passed into her womb." He was born again, and passed for Tuan son of Carell, but the memory of his pre-existence and all his transformations and all the history of Ireland that he witnessed since the days of Partholan still remained with him, and he taught all these things to the Christian monks, who carefully preserved them.

We have now to add some details of the sketch of the successive colonizations of Ireland outlined by Tuan mac Carell.

THE NEMEDIANS

The Nemedians, like the Partholians, came from the mysterious regions of the dead, and both had to do constant battle with the Fomorians. Nemed fought victoriously against them in four great battles, but shortly afterwards died of a plague. The Fomorians were then enabled to establish their tyranny over Ireland. They had at this period two kings, Morc and Conann. The stronghold of the Formorian power was on Tory Island off the coast of Donegal. They extracted a crushing tribute from the people of Ireland, two-thirds of all the milk and two-thirds of the children of the land. At last the Nemedians rose in revolt. Led by three chiefs, they landed on Tory Island, captured Conann's Tower, and Conann himself fell by the hand of the Nemedian chief, Fergus. But Morc at this moment came into the battle with a fresh host, and utterly routed the Nemedians, who were all slain but thirty.

The thirty survivors left Ireland in despair. According to the most ancient belief, they perished utterly, but later accounts represent one family, that of the chief Britan, as settling in Great Britain and giving their name to that country, while two others returned to Ireland under different names, after many wanderings, as the Firbolgs and People of Dana.

THE COMING OF THE FIRBOLGS

The name Firbolgs appears to mean "Men of the Bags", and a legend was invented to account for it. It was said that after settling in Greece, they were set by the people of that country to carry earth from the fertile valleys up to the rocky hills. They did their task by means of leather bags, but at last, growing weary of the oppression, they made boats or coracles out of their bags, and set sail in them for Ireland. Another account says they came from Spain, in three groups; the Fir-Bolg, the Fir-Domnan and the Galioin, who are all generally designated as Firbolgs.

One of their kings, Eochymac Erc, took in marriage Taltiu, or Telta, daughter of the King of the "Great Plain" (the Land of the Dead).

THE COMING OF THE PEOPLE OF DANA

The People of Dana, or *Tuatha De Danann*, were the descendants of Dana, also known as Brigit, a goddess held in much honour by pagan Ireland, whose attributes are in a great measure transferred in legend to the Christian St. Brigit of the sixth century. She was the daughter of the supreme head of the People of Dana, the god Dagda, "The Good". She had three sons, who are said to have had in common one only son, named Ecne—that is to say, "Knowledge", or "Poetry".

The Danaans sprang from four great cities, Falias, Gorias, Finias and Murias. Here they learned science and craftsmanship from great sages, one of whom was enthroned in each city, and from each they brought with them a magical treasure. From Falias came the stone called the *Lia Fail*, or Stone of Destiny, on which the High Kings of Ireland stood when they were crowned, and which was supposed to confirm the election of a rightful monarch by roaring under him as he took his place on it. (An ancient prophecy told that wherever this stone was, a king of the Scotic, or Irish-Milesian, race should reign. This is the famous Stone of Scone, which never came back to Ireland, but was removed to England by Edward I in 1297, and is now the Coronation Stone in Westminster Abbey.)

The second treasure of the Danaans was the invincible sword of Lugh of the Long Arm, and this sword came from the city of Gorias. From Finias came a magic spear, and from Murias the Cauldron of the Dagda, a vessel which had the property that it could feed a host of men without ever being emptied.

The People of Dana were wafted into the land in a magic cloud, making their first appearance in Western Connacht. When the cloud cleared away, the Firbolgs discovered them in a camp which they had already fortified at Moyrein.

The Firbolgs now sent out one of their warriors to interview the mysterious

St. Brigit's Well, Co. Clare. Like many other Celtic deities, the ancient goddess Brigit was incorporated into Christian teaching and her sacred springs were renamed accordingly.

The Coronation Chair, Westminster Abbey, was said to cover the Stone of Destiny, a magical treasure conferred on the Irish people by the Danaans.

"The two ambassadors examined each other's weapons with great interest." (Illustration by Stephen Reid from Rolleston, Myths of the Celtic Race, 1911.)

new-comers, and the People of Dana, on their side, sent a warrior to represent them. The two ambassadors examined each other's weapons with great interest. The spears of the Danaans were light and sharp-pointed; those of the Firbolgs were heavy and blunt.

It was proposed by the Danaans that the two races should divide Ireland equally between them, and join to defend it against all comers for the future. They then exchanged weapons and returned each to his own camp.

The Firbolgs, however, decided to refuse the offer. The battle was joined on the Plain of Moytura, in the south of Co. Mayo, near the spot now called Cong. The Firbolgs were led by their king, mac Erc, and the Danaans by Nuada of the Silver Hand, who got his name from an incident in this battle. His hand, it is said, was cut off in the fight, and one of the skilful artificers who abandoned in the ranks of the Danaans made him a new one of silver. By their magical and healing arts the Danaans gained the victory, and the Firbolg king was slain. But a reasonable agreement followed: the Firbolgs were allotted the province of Connacht for their territory, while the Danaans took the rest of Ireland.

Nuada of the Silver Hand should now have been ruler of the Danaans, but no blemished man might be a king in Ireland. The Danaans therefore chose Bres, son of a Danaan woman named Eri, to reign over them instead. Now Bres had no gift of kingship, for he not only allowed the Fomorians to renew their oppression in the land, but he himself taxed his subjects heavily, and was so niggardly that he gave no hospitality to chiefs and nobles and harpers. One day, it is said, there came to his court the poet Corpry, who found himself housed in a small, dark chamber without fire or furniture, where, after long delay, he was served with three dry cakes and no ale. In revenge he composed a satirical quatrain on his churlish host. Poetic satire in Ireland was supposed to have a kind of magical power. This quatrain of Corpry's was repeated with delight among the people, and Bres had to lay down his sovereignty. This was said to be the first satire ever made in Ireland. Meantime, because Nuada had got his silver hand, he was chosen to be king in place of Bres.

The latter now betook himself in resentment to his mother. Eri declared to him that his father was Elatha, a king of the Formorians, who had come to her secretly from over sea, and when he departed had given her a ring, bidding her never bestow it on any man save him whose finger it would fit. She now brought forth the ring, and it fitted the finger of Bres, and they sailed together for his father's home.

Elatha recognized the ring, and gave his son an army wherewith to reconquer Ireland, and also sent him to seek further aid from the greatest of the Fomorian kings, Balor, surnamed "of the Evil Eye", because the gaze of his one eye could slay those on whom he looked in anger. He was now, however, so old and feeble that the vast eyelid had to be lifted up by his men with ropes and pulleys when the time came to turn it on his foes.

A new figure now comes into the myth, no other than Lugh, son of Kian, the Sun-god of all Celtica, whose name we can still identify in many historic sites on the Continent. (Lyons, Leyden and Laon all derive their names from Lugdunum, the Fortress of Lugh.)

Ballymacgibbon Cairn, Co. Mayo, stands as a monument to the First Battle of Moytura between the Firbolgs and the invading forces of the People of Dana.

Cong, Co. Mayo, on the shores of Lough Corrib, once the scene of the epic battle of Moytura, has since become better known as the location for John Ford's film *The Quiet Man*.

Tory Island, nine miles off the north-west coast of Donegal, is full of ancient ruins, including a prehistoric stronghold known locally as Balor's Fort.

The winged calf (opposite) is used as a symbol of St Luke in the Book of Kells, a magnificently decorated version of the four Gospels made around the beginning of the ninth century.

The story goes that Balor, the Fomorian king, heard in a Druidic prophecy that he would be slain by his grandson. His only child was an infant daughter named Ethlinn. To avert the doom he had her imprisoned in a high tower on a precipitous headland, the Tor Mōr, in Tory Island. He placed the girl in charge of twelve matrons, and in this seclusion Ethlinn grew up into a maiden of surpassing beauty.

Now it happened that there were on the mainland three brothers, namely, Kian, Sawan, and Goban the Smith, the great armourer. Kian had a magical cow, whose milk was so abundant that everyone longed to possess her, and he had to keep her strictly under protection.

Balor determined to possess himself of this cow. One day Kian and Sawan had come to the forge to have some weapons made for them. Kian went into the forge, leaving Sawan in charge of the cow. Balor now appeared on the scene, taking on himself the form of a little red-headed boy, and tricked Sawan into leaving the cow in his care. Balor immediately carried off the cow, and dragged her across the sea to Tory Island.

Kian now determined to avenge himself on Balor, and to this end sought the advice of a Druidess named Birōg. Dressing himself in woman's garb, he was wafted by magic across the sea, where Birōg, who accompanied him, told Ethlinn's guardians that they were two noble ladies escaping from an abductor, and begged for shelter. They were admitted; the matrons were laid by Birōg under the spell of an enchanted slumber, and when they awoke, Kian and the Druidess had vanished as they came. But Ethlinn had given Kian her love, and in due time she was delivered of three sons at a birth.

News of this event came to Balor, and in anger and fear he commanded the

Gold stater of the Atrebates, a Celtic tribe living in northern Gaul which moved to southern Britain after the Roman invasion. Horses were among the most common decorations on Celtic coins. The reverse side of the same coin shows a cross-like abstract pattern. Since trade was conducted mostly by barter, such valuable coins were probably hoarded as evidence of wealth.

three infants to be drowned. The messenger who was charged with this command rolled up the children in a sheet, but the pin of the sheet came loose, and one of the children dropped out and fell into a little bay. The other two were duly drowned, and the servant reported his mission accomplished.

The child who had fallen into the bay was guarded by the Druidess, who wafted it to the home of its father, Kian. He gave it in fosterage to his brother the smith, who taught the child his own trade and made it skilled in every manner of craft. This child was Lugh. When he was grown to a youth the Danaans placed him in charge of Duach, "The Dark", king of the Great Plain (the Land of the Dead), and here he dwelt till he reached manhood.

Then he came to take service with Nuada of the Silver Hand, and when the doorkeeper at the royal palace of Tara asked him what he could do, he answered that he was a carpenter.

"We are in no need of a carpenter," said the door-keeper. "I am a smith too," said Lugh. "We have a master-smith," said the doorkeeper, "already." Lugh went on to name all the occupations and arts he could think of, always receiving the answer that a man of supreme accomplishment in that art was already installed at the court.

"Then ask the King," said Lugh, "if he has in his service any one man who is accomplished in every one of these arts, and if he has, I shall stay here no longer, nor seek to enter his palace." Upon this, Lugh was received and the surname Ildánach was conferred upon him, meaning "The All-Craftsman", while another name that he bore was Lugh Lamfada, or Lugh of the Long Arm.

When Lugh came from the Land of the Living he brought with him many magical gifts. There was the Boat of Mananan, son of Lir the Sea God, which knew a man's thoughts and would travel whithersoever he would, and the Horse of Mananan, that could go alike over land and sea, and a terrible sword named *Fragarach* ("The Answerer"), that could cut through any mail.

Lugh, on his side, prepared for combat against the Fomorians, but to ensure victory, certain magical instruments were still needed for him, and these had now to be obtained. Lugh sent his father Kian northward to summon the fighting men of the Danaans in Ulster. On his way, he met with three brothers, Brian, Iuchar and Iucharba, sons of Turenn, between whose house and that of Kian there was a blood-feud. He sought to avoid them by changing into the form of a pig and joining a herd which was rooting in the plain, but the brothers detected him and Brian wounded him with a cast from a spear. Kian, knowing that his end had come, begged to be allowed to change back into human form before he was slain. "I had rather kill a man than a pig," said Brian. Kian then stood before them as a man, with the blood from Brian's spear trickling from his breast. "I have outwitted you," he cried, "for if you had slain a pig you would have paid but the blood-fine of a pig, but now you shall pay the fine of a man, and the weapons you slay me with shall tell the tale to the avenger of blood."

"Then you shall be slain with no weapons at all," said Brian, and he and the brothers stoned him to death and buried him in the ground as deep as the height of a man.

The invincible sword of Lugh of the Long Arm. Bronze shield and sword found in the River Witham, Lincolnshire. (Illustration from Kembles, Franks and Latham, *Horae Ferales*, 1863.)

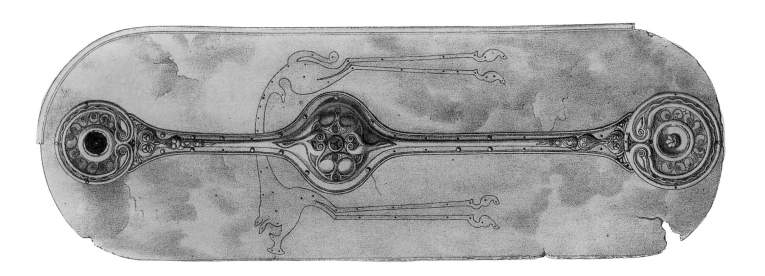

But when Lugh shortly afterwards passed that way the stone on the plain cried out and told him of his father's murder. He uncovered the body, and, vowing vengeance, returned to Tara. Here he accused the sons of Turenn before the High King, and was permitted to have them executed, or to name the fine he would accept in remission of that sentence. Lugh chose the fine, and he named three apples, the skin of a pig, a spear, a chariot with two horses, seven swine, a hound, a cooking-spit, and finally, to give three shouts on a hill. The brothers bound themselves to pay the fine, and Lugh then declared the meaning of it. The apples grew in the Garden of the Sun; the pig-skin was a magical skin which healed every wound and sickness if it could be laid on the sufferer; the spear was a magical weapon owned by the King of Persia; the seven swine belonged to King Asal of the Golden Pillars, and might be killed and eaten every night and yet be found whole next day; the spit belonged to the sea-nymphs of the sunken Island of Finchory; and the three shouts were to

The Island of Finchory, home of the ocean nymphs from whom Brian steals a golden cooking spit. (Illustration by Stephen Reid from T. W. H. Rolleston, *The High Deeds of Finn*, 1910.)

be given on the hill of a fierce warrior, Moachaen, who, with his sons, were under vows to prevent any man from raising his voice on that hill.

The sons of Turenn accomplished, one by one, their tasks, but when all were done save the capture of the cooking-spit and the three shouts, Lugh, by magical arts, caused forgetfulness to fall upon them, and they returned to Ireland with their treasures. These were just what Lugh needed to help him against the Fomorians, but his vengeance was not complete, and he reminded the brothers of what was yet to be won. They now began to understand how they were played with, and went forth sadly. After long wandering they discovered that the Island of Finchory was not above, but under the sea. Brian went down to it, saw the nymphs in their palace, and seized the golden spit from their hearth. The ordeal of the Hill of Mochaen was the last to be attempted. After a desperate combat which ended in the slaying of Mochaen and his sons, the brothers, mortally wounded, uplifted their voices in three faint cries, and so the fine was fulfilled. The life was still in them, however, when they returned to Ireland, and their aged father, Turenn, implored Lugh for the loan of the magic pigskin to heal them, but the implacable Lugh refused, and the brothers and their father died together.

The Second Battle of Moytura took place on a plain in the north of Co. Sligo, which is remarkable for the number of sepulchral monuments still scattered over it. During the battle the craftsmen of the Danaans, Goban the smith, Credné the artificer (or goldsmith) and Luchta the carpenter, kept repairing the broken weapons of the Danaans with magical speed: three blows of Goban's hammer made a spear or sword, Luchta flung a handle at it and it stuck on at once, and Credné jerked the rivets at it with his tongs as fast as he made them, and they flew into their places. The wounded were healed by the magical pigskin.

The Fomorians brought on their champion, Balor, before whose terrible eye Nuada of the Silver Hand and others of the Danaans went down. But Lugh hurled into the eye a great stone and Balor lay dead, as the prophecy had foretold, at the hand of his grandson. The Fomorians were then totally routed, Lugh was enthroned in place of Nuada, and the victory of the solar hero over the powers of darkness and brute force was complete.

The Boat of Mananan took the sons of Turenn to the Garden of the Sun to fetch the three apples. (Illustration by Stephen Reid from T. W. H. Rolleston, *The High Deeds of Finn*, 1910.)

THE COMING OF THE MILESIANS

After the Second Battle of Moytura the Danaans held rule in Ireland until the coming of the Milesians, the sons of Miled. The manner of their coming into Ireland was as follows: Ith, the grandfather of Miled, dwelt in a great tower which his father, Bregon, had built in Spain. One clear winter's day, when looking out westwards, he saw the coast of Ireland in the distance, and resolved to sail to the unknown land. He embarked with ninety warriors, and took land at Corcadyna, in the south-west.

At this time, it is said, Ireland was ruled by three Danaan kings, grandsons of the Dagda. Their names were MacCuill, MacCecht and MacGrené, and their wives were named respectively Banba, Fohla and Eriu. The names of the three goddesses have each at different times been applied to Ireland, but that of the third, Eriu, has alone persisted, and in the dative form, Erinn it continues to be

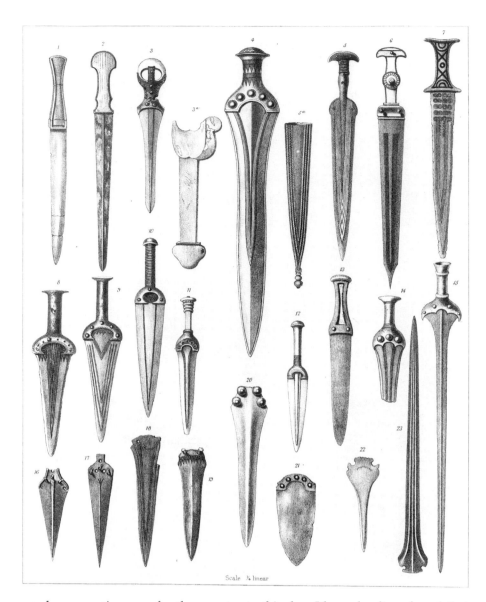

The weapons of the Danaans were repaired during the battle with magical speed by their craftsmen. (Illustration from Kemble, Franks and Latham, *Horae Ferales*, 1863.)

Amergin pronounced judgment. According to Irish fable, the breastplate worn round the neck of a judicial druid would squeeze the wearer's neck if he gave a false judgment. (Illustration from C. Hamilton Smith, *Ancient Costumes of Great Britain and Ireland*, 1814.)

used as a poetic name for the country to this day. Ith, on landing, found that the Danaan king, Neit, had just been slain in a battle with the Fomorians, and the three sons, MacCuill and the others, were at the fortress of Aileach, in Co. Donegal, arranging for a division of the land among themselves. At first they welcomed Ith, and asked him to settle their inheritance. Ith gave his judgment, but, in concluding, his admiration for the newly discovered country broke out: "Act," he said, "according to the laws of justice, for the country you dwell in is a good one." The Danaans concluded that Ith had designs upon their land, and they seized him and put him to death. His companions, however, recovered his body and bore it back with them in their ships to Spain. The children of Miled resolved to take vengeance for the outrage and prepared to invade Ireland. They were commanded by thirty-six chiefs, each having his own ship with his family and his followers.

The Milesian host, after landing, advanced to Tara, where they found the three kings of the Danaans awaiting them, and summoned them to deliver up the island. The Danaans asked for three days' time to consider whether they should quit Ireland, or submit, or give battle, and they proposed to leave the decision, upon their request, to Amergin, the poet and son of Miled. Amergin pronounced judgment. He agreed that the Milesians were not to take their foes by surprise; they were to withdraw the length of nine waves from the shore, and then return; if they then conquered the Danaans the land was to be fairly theirs by right of battle and the Danaans should withdraw.

The Milesians submitted to this decision and embarked on their ships. But no sooner had they drawn off for this mystical distance of the nine waves than a mist and storm were raised by the sorceries of the Danaans. The coast of Ireland was hidden from their sight, and they wandered dispersed upon the ocean.

Amergin, who as poet—that is to say, Druid—took the lead in all critical situations, thereupon chanted his incantation to the land of Erin. The wind fell, and they turned their prows, rejoicing, towards the shore. But one of the Milesian lords, Eber Donn, exulted in brutal rage at the prospect of putting all the dwellers in Ireland to the sword; the tempest immediately sprang up again, and many of the Milesian ships foundered, Eber Donn's being among them. At last a remnant of the Milesians found their way to shore, and landed in the estuary of the Boyne.

A great battle with the Danaans at Telltown then followed. The three kings and three queens of the Danaans, with many of their people, were slain, and the children of Miled—the last of the mythical invaders of Ireland—entered upon the sovereignty of Ireland. But the People of Dana did not withdraw. By their magic art they cast over themselves a veil of invisibility, which they could put on or off as they chose. There were two Irelands henceforward, the spiritual and the earthly. The Danaans dwelt in the spiritual Ireland, which was portioned out among them by their great overlord, the Dagda. Where the human eye could see but green mounds and ramparts, the relics of ruined fortresses or sepulchres, there rose the fair palaces of the defeated divinities; there they held their revels in eternal sunshine, nourished by the magic meat and ale that gave them undying youth and beauty; and thence they came forth at times to mingle with mortal men in love or in war.

Spiritual Ireland, the home of the Danaans, could be entered through the gateways formed by ancient burial chambers. Kilclooney More portal tomb, near Narin, Co. Donegal.

Tara, view from the Hill of Kings, Co. Meath. Traditional residence of the high kings of Ireland, the hill commands views across the central Irish plain to the east Galway mountains, over a hundred miles away.

The Children of Lir, by John Duncan
(1866–1945). Transformed by sorcery into
four white swans, Lir's children were
condemned to a life of hardship. (Dundee
Art Galleries and Museums.)

THE CHILDREN OF LIR

When Christianity came to Ireland, the people of Dana were often shown as
supernatural beings redeemed by the new religion and given eternal life in a
Christian heaven. Such is the case with the tale of the children of Lir, which is
often classified as one of the "Three Sorrowful Tales of Erin". It is not known
exactly how old this tale is, since the earliest written versions that survive are
less than 300 years old.

Lir was a Danaan divinity, the father of the sea-god Mananan. He had married in succession two sisters, the second of whom was named Aoife. She was
childless, but the former wife of Lir had left him four children, a girl named
Fionuala and three younger boys called Aod, Fiachra and Conn. The intense
love of Lir for the children made the stepmother jealous, and she ultimately
resolved on their destruction.

With her guilty object in view, Aoife went on a journey to a neighbouring
Danaan king, Bov the Red, taking the four children with her. Arriving at a
lonely place by Lake Derryvaragh, in Westmeath, she ordered her attendants
to slay the children. They refused, and rebuked her. Then she resolved to do it

herself, but instead of killing the children, she transformed them by sorcery into four white swans, and laid on them the following doom: three hundred years they were to spend on the waters of Lake Derryvaragh, three hundred on the Straits of Moyle (between Ireland and Scotland), and three hundred on the Atlantic by Erris and Inishglory. After that, "when the woman of the South is mated with the man of the North", the enchantment was to end.

When the children failed to arrive with Aoife at the palace of Bov, her guilt was discovered, and Bov changed her into "a demon of the air". She flew forth shrieking, and was heard of no more in the tale. But Lir and Bov sought out the swan-children, and found that they had not only human speech, but had preserved the characteristic Danaan gift of making wonderful music. From all parts of the island, companies of the Danaan folk resorted to Lake Derryvaragh to hear this wondrous music and to converse with the swans, and during that time a great peace and gentleness seemed to pervade the land.

But at last the day came for them to take up their life by the wild cliffs and angry sea of the northern coast. Forbidden to land, their feathers froze to the rocks in the winter nights, and they were often buffeted and driven apart by storms.

Fionuala, the eldest of the four, took the lead in all their doings, and mothered the younger children most tenderly, wrapping her plumage round them on nights of frost. At last the time came to enter on the third and last period of their doom, and they took flight for the western shores of Mayo. Here, too, they suffered much hardship, but the Milesians had now come into the land, and a young farmer named Ervic, dwelling on the shores of Erris Bay, found out who and what the swans were, and befriended them. To him they told their story, and through him it is supposed to have been preserved and handed down. When the final period of their suffering was close at hand, they resolved to fly towards the palace of their father Lir, who dwelt, we are told, at the Hill of the White Field, in Armagh, to see how things had fared with him. They did so, but not knowing what had happened on the coming of the Milesians, they were shocked and bewildered to find nothing but green mounds where once stood—and still did, only that they could not see it—the palace of their father.

On Erris Bay they heard for the first time the sound of a Christian bell. It came from the chapel of a hermit who had established himself there. The swans were at first startled and terrified by the thin, dreadful sound, but afterwards approached and made themselves known to the hermit, who instructed them in the faith.

Now it happened that a princess of Munster, Deoca, (the "woman of the South") became betrothed to a Connacht chief named Lairgnen, and begged him for a wedding gift to procure for her the four wonderful singing swans. He asked them of the hermit, who refused to give them up, whereupon the "man of the North" seized them violently by the silver chains with which the hermit had coupled them, and dragged them off to Deoca. This was their last trial. Arrived in her presence, an awful transformation befell them. The swan plumage fell off, and revealed four withered human beings, shrunken in the decrepitude of their vast old age. Lairgnen flew from the place in horror, but the hermit prepared to administer baptism at once, as death was rapidly approaching them. "Lay us in one grave," said Fionuala. And so it was done, and they went to heaven.

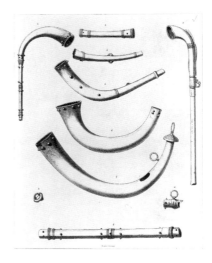

The Danaan gift of making wonderful music. Although trumpets like these were used to frighten the enemy in battle, the Celts made more gentle music with harps strung with hair. (Illustration from Kemble, Franks and Latham, *Horae Ferales*, 1863.)

CHAPTER III

THE EARLY MILESIAN KINGS

The kings and heroes of the Milesian race now fill the foreground of the stage in Irish legendary history. But, although banished to the other world, the Danaan divinities are by no means forgotten. The fairyland in which they dwell is ever near at hand; the invisible barriers may be, and often are, crossed by mortal men, and the Danaans themselves frequently come forth from them. Yet whatever the Danaans may have been in the original pre-Christian conceptions of the Celtic Irish, it would be a mistake to suppose that they figure in the legends, as these have now come down to us, in the light of gods as we understand this term. They are for the most part beautiful, immortal (with limitations), and they wield mysterious powers of sorcery, but no sort of moral governance of the world is ever for a moment ascribed to them, nor (in the bardic literature) is any act of worship paid to them. They do not die naturally, but they can be slain both by each other and by mortals, and on the whole, the mortal race is the stronger. The early kings and heroes of the Milesian race are, indeed, often represented as so mightily endowed with supernatural power that it is impossible to draw a clear distinction between them and the People of Dana in this respect.

Poulnabron Dolmen stands in the Burren, an area of underground caves, streams and potholes, where Arctic plants grow alongside Mediterranean flowers and it is easy to imagine that magical powers are at work.

Etain (opposite), the most beautiful woman in Ireland, inspired some of the most lyrical descriptions in early Irish literature. *Etain, Helen, Maeve and Fand* by Harry Clarke. (Illustration from J. M. Synge, *Queens*.)

THE MILESIAN SETTLEMENT OF IRELAND

The Milesians had three leaders when they set out for the conquest of Ireland—Eber Downn (Brown Eber), Eber Finn (Fair Eber), and Eremon. Of these the first-named was not allowed to enter the land; he perished as a punishment for his brutality. When the victory over the Danaans was secure, the two remaining brothers turned to the Druid Amergin for a judgment as to their respective titles to the sovereignty. Eremon was the elder of the two, but Eber refused to submit to him. Amergin decided that the land should belong to Eremon for his life, and pass to Eber after his death. But Eber demanded an immediate partition of the new-won territory. This was agreed to, and Eber took the

The Paps of Anu. These hills in Co. Kerry were named after Anu, or Dana, mother goddess and ancestor of the Danaans, who represent the otherworld in Irish myth.

The High King at Tara owed his authority partly to fact that the hill had been a sacred site for centuries. Carvings in the passage grave known as the Mound of Hostages at Tara date from around 1800 B.C.

southern half of Ireland, while Eremon occupied the north. But even so, the brethren could not be at peace, and war broke out between them. Eber was slain, and Eremon became sole King of Ireland, which he ruled from Tara.

Of the kings who succeeded Eremon, and the battles they fought and the forests they cleared away, and the rivers and lakes that broke out in their reign, there is little to record till we come to the reign of Tiernmas, fifth in succession from Eremon. He is said to have introduced into Ireland the worship of Crom Cruach, on Moyslaught (The Plain of Adoration), and to have perished himself with three-fourths of his people while worshipping this idol on November Eve, the period when the reign of winter was inaugurated. Tiernmas also, it is said, found the first gold-mine in Ireland, and introduced variegated colours into the clothing of the people. A slave might wear but one colour, a peasant two, a soldier three, a wealthy landowner four, a provincial chief five, and an Ollav six. Ollav was a term applied to a certain Druidic rank. It is a characteristic trait that the Ollav is endowed with a distinction equal to that of a king.

The most distinguished Ollav of Ireland was also a king, the celebrated Ollav Fōla, who is supposed to have been eighteenth from Eremon and to have reigned about 1000 B.C. He gave the country a code of legislature, and subdivided it, under the High King at Tara, among the provincial chiefs, to each of whom his proper rights and obligations were allotted. To Ollav Fōla is also attributed the foundation of the great triennial Festival at Tara, where the sub-kings and chiefs, bards, historians, and musicians from all parts of Ireland assembled to make up the genealogical records of the clan chieftainships, to enact laws, hear disputed cases, settle succession, and so forth. It was a stringent law that at this season all enmities must be laid aside; no man might lift his hand against another, or even institute a legal process, during the period that the Assembly at Tara was in progress.

The next king who comes into legendary prominence is Ugainy the Great, who is said to have ruled not only all Ireland, but a great part of Western Europe, and to have wedded a Gaulish princess named Kesair. He had two sons, Laery and Covac. The former inherited the kingdom, but Covac, sick with envy, sought to slay him, and asked the advice of a Druid as to how this could be managed, since Laery never would visit him without an armed escort. The Druid bade him feign death, and have word sent to his brother that he was ready for burial. This Covac did, and when Laery arrived and bent over the supposed corpse, Covac stabbed him to the heart, and slew also one of his sons, Ailill, who attended him. Then Covac ascended the throne, and straightway his illness left him.

LEGENDS OF MAON, SON OF AILILL

He did a brutal deed, however, upon a son of Ailill's, named Maon, who, as a child, was brought into Covac's presence, and was there compelled to swallow a portion of his father's and grandfather's hearts, and also a mouse with her young. From the disgust he felt, the child lost his speech, and Covac let him go. The boy was then taken into Munster, to the kingdom of Feramorc, and remained with him some time, but afterwards went to Gaul, his great-grandmother Kesair's country, where he was treated with great honour and grew up into a noble youth. But he left behind him in the heart of Moriath, daughter of the King of Feramorc, a passion that could not be stilled, and she resolved to

An Irish Ollav or Ollamh was entitled to wear clothes of six colours, a distinction which placed him above all other ranks of society except the high king. (Illustration from C. Hamilton Smith, *Ancient Costumes of Great Britain and Ireland*, 1814.)

The worship of Crom Cruach is said to have entailed human sacrifice. Evidence of head cults, such as this third-century B.C. doorway with skulls from a sanctuary in Roquepertuse, France, may have contributed to such stories.

bring him back to Ireland. She accordingly equipped her father's harper, Craftiny, with many rich gifts, and wrote for him a love-lay, in which her passion for Maon was set forth. Arrived in France, Craftiny made his way to the king's court, and found occasion to pour out his lay to Maon. So deeply stirred was he by the beauty and passion of the song that his speech returned to him. The King of Gaul then equipped him with an armed force and sent him to Ireland to regain his kingdom. Learning that Covac was at a place near at hand named Dinrigh, Maon and his body of Gauls made a sudden attack upon him and slew him there and then, with all his nobles and guards. After the slaughter, a Druid of Covac's company asked one of the Gauls who their leader was. "The Mariner", replied the Gaul, meaning the captain of the fleet, Maon. "Can he speak?" inquired the Druid, who had begun to suspect the truth. "He does speak," said the man and henceforth the name "Labra the Mariner" clung to Maon, son of Ailill, nor was he known by any other. He then sought out Moriath, wedded her, and reigned over Ireland ten years.

LEGEND-CYCLE OF CONARY MŌR

We now come to a cycle of legends centering on, or rather closing with, the wonderful figure of the High King Conary Mōr.

Etain

The Ipswich torcs, gold neck rings made of finely wrought metal, date from the first century B.C. Such fine jewellery might be offered as a sacrifice to the gods, as well as being worn. (British Museum.)

The preliminary events of the cycle took place in the "Land of Youth". Midir the Proud, son of the Dagda, had a wife named Fuamnach. After a while he took to himself another bride, Etain, whose beauty and grace were beyond compare. Fuamnach became jealous of her rival, changed her into a butterfly,

The River Boyne is supposed to have its source in the well of the Tuatha de Danaan. At Brugh na Boinne (the bend in the Boyne) stands the mound of New Grange.

The Ogham Stone at Castlestrange, Co. Roscommon, is similar in shape and in its carvings to the navel stone at Delphi in Greece, the legendary centre of the world.

raised a tempest that drove her forth from the palace, and kept her for seven years buffeted throughout the length and breadth of Erin. At last, however, a gust of wind blew her through a window of the fairy palace of Angus on the Boyne. Unable to release her altogether from the spell of Fuamnach, he made a sunny bower for her, while in the secrecy of the night he restored her to her own form and enjoyed her love. In time, however, her refuge was discovered by Fuamnach; again the magic tempest drove her forth. Blown into the palace of an Ulster chieftain named Etar, she fell into the drinking-cup of Etar's wife, just as the latter was about to drink. She was swallowed in the draught, and in due time, having passed into the womb of Etar's wife, she was born as an apparently mortal child, and grew up to maidenhood knowing nothing of her real nature and ancestry.

About this time it happened that the High King of Ireland, Eochy, being wifeless and urged by the nobles of his land to take a queen, sent forth to inquire for a fair and noble maiden to share his throne. The messengers reported that Etain, daughter of Etar, was the fairest maiden in Ireland, and the king journeyed forth to visit her. Eochy found Etain with her maidens by a spring of water, whither she had gone forth to wash her hair. Her hair was golden yellow and her skin as white as new-fallen snow. Never a maid more worthy of love was till then seen by the eyes of men, and it seemed to them that she must be one of those that have come from the fairy mounds. The king wooed her and made her his wife, and brought her back to Tara.

It happened that the king had a brother named Ailill, who, on seeing Etain, was so smitten with her beauty that he fell sick, wasted almost to death. While he was in this condition, Eochy had to make a royal progress through Ireland. He left his brother in Etain's care, bidding her do what she could for him, and, if he died, to bury him with due ceremonies and erect an Ogham stone above his grave to mark the place. Etain went to visit the brother, and he broke out in an avowal of his passion for her.

Etain was now in some perplexity; but she decided that although she was not in the least in love with Ailill, she could not see a man die of longing for her, and she promised that she would become his.

She arranged a tryst with Ailill in a house outside of Tara, for she would not do what she called her "glorious crime" in the king's palace. But Ailill on the eve of the appointed day fell into a profound slumber and missed his appointment. A being in his shape did, however, come to Etain, but merely to speak coldly and sorrowfully of his malady, and depart again. When the two met once more the situation was altogether changed. In Ailill's enchanted sleep, his unholy passion for the queen had passed entirely away. Etain, on the other hand, became aware that behind the visible events there are mysteries which she did not understand.

The explanation soon followed. The being who came to her in the shape of Ailill was her Danaan husband, Midir the Proud. He now came to woo her in his true shape, and entreated her to fly with him to the Land of Youth, where she might be safe henceforward, since her persecutor, Fuamnach, was dead. He it was who shed upon Ailill's eyes the magic slumber.

Etain, however, was by no means ready to go away with a stranger and to desert the High King for a man without name or lineage. Midir told her who he was, and all her own history of which, in her present incarnation, she knew nothing. Ultimately Etain agreed to return with Midir to her ancient home, but only on condition that the king would agree to their severance, and with this Midir had to be content for the time.

The Desborough mirror, dating from the first century B.C., is patterned with swirls and coils inspired by natural branches and leaves. It would have been the property of a wealthy woman. (British Museum.)

The Mound of Hostages at Tara still retains its original earth covering, unlike many prehistoic burial chambers. Such well-preserved mounds were often seen as fairy palaces.

Midir and Etain. "The couple rose lightly in the air and disappeared." (Illustration by Stephen Reid from T. W. H. Rolleston, *The High Deeds of Finn*, 1910.)

Shortly afterwards, he appeared to King Eochy on the Hill of Tara. He told the king that he had come to play a game of chess with him, and produced a chessboard of silver with pieces of gold, studded with jewels.

Eochy entered into the game with zest. Midir allowed him to win game after game, and in payment for his losses, he performed by magic all kinds of tasks for Eochy, reclaiming land, clearing forests, and building causeways across bogs. At last, having excited Eochy's cupidity and made him believe himself the better player, he proposed a final game, the stakes to be at the pleasure of the victor after the game was over. Eochy was defeated.

"What is it that you desire me to grant?" said Eochy.

"That I may hold Etain in my arms and obtain a kiss from her," said Midir.

The king was silent for a while; then he said "One month from to-day you will come, and the thing you desire shall be granted you."

When the appointed day came, Eochy caused the palace of Tara to be surrounded by a great host of armed men to keep Midir out. All was in vain, however; as the king sat at the feast, Midir, more glorious than ever, suddenly stood in their midst. Holding his spears in his left hand, he threw his right around Etain, and the couple rose lightly in the air and disappeared through a roof-window in the palace. The king and his warriors rushed out of doors, but all they could see were two white swans that circled in the air above the palace, and then departed towards the fairy mountain of Slievenamon. And thus Queen Etain left the land of men and rejoined her kindred.

Eochy, however, would not accept defeat, and after searching Ireland for his wife in vain, he summoned to his aid the Druid Dalan. Dalan tried for a year by every means in his power to find out where she was. At last he made three wands of yew, and upon the wands he wrote an ogham, and by the keys of wisdom that he had, and by the ogham, it was revealed to him that Etain was in the fairy mound of Bri-Leith.

Eochy then assembled his forces to storm and destroy the fairy mound in which was the palace of Midir. At last Midir, driven to the last stronghold, attempted a stratagem—he offered to give up Etain, and sent her with fifty handmaids to the king, but made them all so much alike that Eochy could not distinguish the true Etain from her images. She herself gave him a sign by which to know her. By this means Eochy regained his queen, who lived with him till his death, ten years afterwards, and bore him one daughter, who was named Etain, like herself.

The Tale of Conary Mōr

From this Etain ultimately sprang the great king Conary Mōr, whose overthrow and death were compassed by the Danaans in vengeance for the devastation of their sacred dwellings by Eochy. The genealogy of Conary Mōr will help the reader to understand the connexion of events.

Eochy = Etain.

Cormac, King = Etain Oig (Etain the younger).
of Ulster.

Eterskel, King = Messbuachalla (the cowherd's
of Erin   fosterling).

Conary Mōr.

The tale of Conary introduces us for the first time to the law or institution of the *geis*, which plays a very important part in Irish legend, the violation or observance of a *geis* being frequently the turning-point in a tragic narrative.

Dineen's "Irish Dictionary" explains the word *geis* as meaning "a bond, a spell, a prohibition, a taboo, a magical injunction, the violation of which led to misfortune and death." Every Irish chieftain or personage of note had certain *geise* peculiar to himself which he must not transgress. It is not at all clear who imposed these *geise* or how any one found out what his personal *geise* were, but they were regarded as sacred obligations.

We now return to follow the fortunes of Etain's great-grandson, Conary. Her daughter, Etain Oig married Cormac, King of Ulster. She bore her husband no children save one daughter only. Embittered by her barrenness, the king put away Etain, and ordered her infant to be thrown into a pit. Then his two thralls took her to a pit, and she smiled a laughing smile at them as they were putting her into it. After that they could not leave her to die, and they carried her to a cowherd of Eterskel, King of Tara, by whom she was fostered and taught till she became a good embroidress, and there was not in Ireland a king's daughter dearer than she. Hence the name she bore, Messbuachalla, which means "the cowherd's foster-child".

A bull-feast was held. The base plate from the silver-gilt ritual cauldron found at Gundestrup in Denmark shows a giant bull apparently being sacrificed by a god or priest. (National Museum of Denmark.)

For fear of her being discovered, the cowherd kept the maiden in a house of wickerwork, having only a roof-opening. But one of King Eterskel's folk had the curiosity to climb up and look in, and saw there the fairest maiden in Ireland. He bore word to the king, who ordered an opening to be made in the wall and the maiden fetched forth and taken to the king, for Eterskel was childless, and it had been prophesied to him by his Druid that a woman of unknown race would bear him a son.

Before her release, however, she was visited by a great bird which came down through her roof-window. On the floor of the hut, his plumage fell from him and revealed a glorious youth. Like Leda, like Ethlinn, daughter of Balor, she gave her love to the god. Before they parted, he told her that she would be taken to the king, but that she would bear to her Danaan lover a son whose name was to be Conary, and that it should be forbidden to him when he grew up to go a-hunting after any kind of bird.

So Conary was born, and grew up into a wise and noble youth, and he was fostered with a lord named Desa, whose three great-grandsons grew up with him from childhood.

Then King Eterskel died, and a successor had to be appointed. In Ireland the eldest son did not succeed to the throne as a matter of right, but a bull-feast was held. A bull was slain, and the diviner would eat his fill and drink its broth; then he went to bed, where a truth-compelling spell was chanted over him. Whoever he saw in his dream would be king. The dreamer cried in his sleep that he saw a naked man going towards Tara with a stone in his sling.

The bull feast was held at Tara, but Conary was then with his three foster-brothers playing a game on the Plains of Liffey. They separated, Conary going towards Dublin, where he saw before him a flock of great birds. He drove after them in his chariot, but the birds never let him come up with them till they reached the sea-shore. Then he lighted down from his chariot and took out his sling to cast at them, whereupon they changed into armed men and turned on him with spears and swords. One of them, however, protected him, and said: "I am Nemglan, king of your father's birds, and you have been forbidden to cast at birds, for here there is no one but is thy kin. Go to Tara to-night, the bull-feast is there, and through it you will be made king."

So Conary stripped off his raiment and went naked through the night to Tara, where all the roads were being watched by chiefs. When Conary met them they clothed him and brought him in, and he was proclaimed King of Erin. Nemglan also told Conary his *geise*, none of which he might transgress for fear of incurring disaster or even death: "Thou shalt not go right-handwise round Tara, nor left-handwise round Bregia. Thou shalt not go out every ninth night beyond Tara. Thou shalt not sleep in a house from which firelight shows after sunset, or in which light can be seen from without. No three Reds shall go before thee to the house of Red. After sunset, no one woman alone or man alone shall enter the house in which thou art."

Conary then entered upon his reign, which was marked by fair seasons and bounteous harvests. Foreign ships came to the ports. No one slew another and to every one his fellow's voice seemed as sweet as the strings of lutes. From mid-spring to mid-autumn no wind disturbed a cow's tail.

Disturbance, however, came from another source. Conary had put down all raiding and rapine, but his three foster-brothers pursued their evil ways and were at last captured red-handed. Conary would not condemn them to death, but banished them from Erin. On the seas they met another exiled chief, Ingcel the One-Eyed, son of the King of Britain, and joining forces with him they attacked the fortress in which Ingcel's father, mother and brothers were guests at the time, and all were destroyed. It was then the turn of Ingcel to ask their help in raiding the land of Erin, and gathering a host of other outlawed men, they made a descent upon Ireland. Meantime Conary had been lured by the machinations of the Danaans into breaking one after another of his *geise*. He settled a quarrel between two of his serfs in Munster, and travelling back to Tara they saw the country around it lit with the glare of fires and wrapped in clouds of smoke. A host from the North, they thought, must be raiding the

Leda by Cesare da Sesto, after Leonardo, *c.* 1520 (Wilton House). "Like Leda, like Eithlinn daughter of Balor, she gave her love to the god."

Howth, an island on the shores of Dublin Bay, takes its name from the Norse word *hoved*, meaning head. It was the site of the first Viking invasions in the ninth century.

British Fishing and Husbandry. Although most of their tales concern war and conflict, the Celts were primarily farmers and herdsmen. (Illustration from C. Hamilton Smith, *Ancient Costumes of Great Britain and Ireland*, 1814.)

The number three, a sacred figure to the Celts, occurs in several myths and is represented in carvings of triple heads and in this gold coin from Gaul, modelled on the staters of Philip II of Macdeon.

The charioteer depicted on the other side of the coin is probably derived from Greek images of Apollo, the god of the sun. It was a popular motif on Celtic coins.

country, and to escape it, Conary's company had to turn right-handwise round Tara and then left-handwise round the Plain of Bregia. But the smoke and flames were an illusion made by the Fairy Folk.

Conary had now to find a resting-place for the night, and he recollected that he was not far from the Hostel of the Leinster lord, Da Derga. Conary had been generous to him when Da Derga came visiting to Tara, and he determined to seek his hospitality for the night. As the cavalcade were journeying thither, Conary marked in front of them on the road three horsemen clad all in red and riding on red horses. He remembered his *geis* about the "three Reds," and sent a messenger to bid them fall behind.

But they rode forward, and, alighting from their red steeds fastened them at the portal of Da Derga's Hostel and sat down inside. "Derga" means "red". Despite his efforts to avert such an event Conary had therefore been preceded by three red horsemen to the House of Red.

Night had fallen, and the pirate host of Ingcel was encamped on the shores of Dublin Bay. A crashing noise was heard—it was the giant warrior mac Cecht striking flint on steel to kindle fire for the king's feast. A glare of the fire lit by mac Cecht was now perceived by the pirate host, shining through the wheels of the chariots drawn up around the open doors of the Hostel. Another of the *geise* of Conary had been broken.

In the Hostel, the king was preparing for the night. A solitary woman came to the door and sought admission. It was the Morrigan, the Danaan goddess of Death and Destruction. Conary declared that his *geis* forbade him to receive a solitary man or woman after sunset. "If in truth", she said, "it has befallen the king not to have room in his house for the meal and bed of a solitary woman, they will be gotten apart from him from some one possessing generosity." "Let her in, then," said Conary, "though it is a *geis* of mine."

Ingcel and the sons of Desa then marched to the attack and surrounded the Hostel:

"Silence a while!" said Conary, "What is this?"

"Champions at the house," said Conall of the Victories.

"There are warriors for them here," answered Conary.

"They will be needed to-night," Conall rejoined.

Then the great struggle began. The Hostel was set on fire, but the fire was quenched with wine or any liquids that were in it. Conary and his people sallied forth and the reavers, for the moment, were routed. But Conary was athirst and could do no more till he had water. The reavers had cut off the river Dodder, which formerly flowed through the Hostel, and all the liquids in the house had been spilt on the fires.

The king, who was perishing of thirst, asked mac Cecht to procure him a drink. Mac Cecht then, taking Conary's golden cup, rushed forth, bursting through the surrounding host. Conall, Sencha and Duftach stood by Conary till the end, but mac Cecht was long in returning, Conary perished of thirst, and the three heroes then fought their way out.

Meantime, mac Cecht had rushed over Ireland in frantic search for the water. He tried the great rivers, Shannon and Slayney, Bann and Barrow—they all hid away at his approach. At last he found a Lake, Loch Gara in Roscommon, which failed to hide itself in time, and thereat he filled his cup. In the morning he returned to the Hostel with the draught, but found the defenders all dead or fled, and two of the reavers in the act of striking off the head of Conary. Mac Cecht struck off the head of one of them, and hurled a huge pillar stone after the other, who was escaping with Conary's head. The reaver fell dead on the spot, and mac Cecht, taking up his master's head, poured the water into its mouth. Thereupon the head spoke, and praised and thanked him for the deed.

Conary's golden cup. Found in a princely grave in Schwarzenbach, Germany, this sheet gold openwork casing once housed a bowl probably used as a drinking vessel. (Staatliche Museen zu Berlin.)

51

CHAPTER IV

TALES OF THE ULTONIAN CYCLE

The centre of interest in Irish legend now shifts from Tara to Ulster, and a multitude of heroic tales gather round the Ulster king Conor mac Nessa, round Cuchulain, his great vassal, and the Red Branch Order of chivalry, which had its seat in Emain Macha.

THE FOUNDING OF EMAIN MACHA

Macha was the daughter of Red Hugh, an Ulster prince who had two brothers, Dithorba and Kimbay. The three brothers agreed to enjoy, each in turn, the sovereignty of Ireland. Red Hugh came first, but on his death Macha refused to give up the realm and fought Dithorba for it, whom she conquered and slew. She then compelled Kimbay to wed her and ruled all Ireland as queen.

The five sons of Dithorba fled across the Shannon and plotted against Macha. Then the Queen went alone into Connacht and found the brothers in the forest. One by one she overpowered and bound them. Then she lifted them upon her back and returned with them into the north. With the spear of her brooch she marked out on the plain the circuit of the city of Emain Macha, whose ramparts and trenches were constructed by the captive princes.

Another tale concerning Macha makes her a supernatural being. This legend tells that a wealthy Ulster farmer named Crundchu found one day in his fortress a young woman whom he had never seen before. The strange woman, without a word, took on herself all the duties of the mistress of the household. At night she lay down at Crundchu's side, and thereafter dwelt with him as his wife, and they loved each other dearly. Her name was Macha.

One day Crundchu prepared himself to go to a great fair or assembly of the Ultonians, where there would be merrymaking of all kinds. Macha begged her husband not to go. He persisted. "Then", she said, "at least do not speak of me in the assembly, for I may dwell with you only so long as I am not spoken of."

Crundchu promised to obey the injunction, and went to the festival. Here the two horses of the king carried off prize after prize in the racing, and the

Bronze brooch from Emain Macha.
Popularly supposed to resemble the shape of the hilltop stronghold where it was found. (British Museum.)

Emain Macha (opposite), now known as Navan Fort, is in Co. Armargh. Occupied since between 600 and 100 B.C., this ancient site was for many centuries the seat of the kings of Ulster.

The Curse of Macha was that the Ulstermen should suffer the pangs of childbirth when they most needed to fight. (Illustration from T. W. H. Rolleston, *Myths of the Celtic Race*, 1911.)

people cried: "There is not in Ireland a swifter than the King's pair of horses."

"I have a wife at home," said Crundchu, in a moment of forgetfulness, "who can run quicker than these horses."

"Seize that man," said the angry king, "and hold him till his wife be brought to the contest."

So messengers went for Macha, and she was brought before the assembly, and she was with child. The king bade her prepare for the race. She pleaded her condition. "I am close upon my hour," she said. "Give me but a short delay till I am delivered." But the king and all the crowd would hear of no delay. So she raced against the horses, and outran them, but as she came to the goal she gave a great cry and gave birth to twin children. As she uttered that cry, however, all the spectators felt themselves seized with pangs like her own and had no more strength than a woman in her travail. And Macha prophesied: "From this hour the shame you have wrought on me will fall upon each man of Ulster. In the hours of your greatest need you shall be weak and helpless as women in childbirth, and this shall endure for five days and four nights—to the ninth generation the curse shall be upon you." And so it came to pass, and this was the cause of the Debility of the Ultonians that was wont to afflict the warriors of the province.

CONOR MAC NESSA

The chief occasion on which this Debility was manifested was when Maev, Queen of Connaught, made the famous Cattle-raid of Quelgny (*Tain Bo Cualigné*), which forms the subject of the greatest tale in Irish literature. We have now to relate the preliminary history leading up to this epic tale and introducing its chief characters.

Fachtna the Giant, King of Ulster, had to wife Nessa, daughter of Echid Yellow-heel, and she bore him a son named Conor. But when Fachtna died, Fergus, his half-brother, succeeded him, Conor being then but a youth. Now Fergus loved Nessa, and would have wedded her, but she made conditions. "Let my son Conor reign one year," she said, "so that his posterity may be the descendants of a king, and I consent." Fergus agreed, and young Conor took the throne. But so wise and prosperous was his rule that, at the year's end, the

Becfola, like Maev, Queen of Connacht, belonged to a Celtic tradition of warrior women. (Illustration by Arthur Rackham from James Stephens, *Irish Fairy Tales*, 1920.)

people would have him remain king, and Fergus, who loved the feast and the chase better than the toils of kingship, was content to have it so.

In Conor's time was the glory of the "Red Branch" in Ulster, who were the offspring of Ross the Red, King of Ulster. Ross the Red, it is said, wedded a Danaan woman, Magda, daughter of Angus Og. As a second wife, he wedded a maiden named Roy. His descendants are as follows:

Maga = Ross the Red = Roy

Fachtna = Nessa   Fergus mac Roy
the Giant

Conor mac
Nessa

But Maga was also wedded to the Druid Cathbad, and by him had three daughters.

Cathbad = Maga

Dectera = Lugh   Elva = Usna   Finchoom = Amorgin

Cuchulain   Naisi   Ainlé   Ardan   Conall of the
Victories

CUCHULAIN

It was during the reign of Conor mac Nessa that the birth of the mightiest hero of the Celtic race, Cuchulain, came about. The maiden Dectera, daughter of Cathbad, with fifty young girls, one day disappeared, and for three years no searching availed to discover their dwelling-place or their fate. At last one summer day a flock of birds descended on the fields about Emain Macha and began to destroy the crops. The king, with Fergus and others of his nobles, went out against them with slings, but the birds lured the party on and on till at last they found themselves near the Fairy Mound of Angus on the river Boyne. Night fell, and the king sent Fergus with a party to discover some habitation where they might sleep. One of them came to a noble mansion by the river, and on entering it was met by a young man of splendid appearance. With the stranger was a lovely woman, his wife, and fifty maidens, and he recognized in them Dectera and her maidens, and in the glorious youth Lugh of the Long Arm. He went back with his tale to the king, who immediately sent for Dectera to come to him. She, alleging that she was ill, requested a delay, and so the night passed, but in the morning there was found in the hut among the Ulster warriors a new-born male infant. It was Dectera's gift to Ulster. The child was taken home by the warriors and was given to Dectera's sister, Finchoom, who was then nursing her own child, Conall, and the boy was called Setanta. And the part of Ulster from Dundalk southward to Usna, which is called the Plain of Murthemney, was allotted for his inheritance.

The boy Setanta follows King Conor to the home of Cullan, the wealthy smith of Quelgny. (Illustration from T. W. H. Rolleston, *Myths of the Celtic Race*, 1911.)

The River Boyne represented the southern limit of the kingdom of Ulster and was the legendary birthplace of Cuchulain, son of the sun god Lugh.

Setanta overcame the hound and had then to take its place as guard dog, calling himself Cuchulain or the Hound of Cullan. (Illustration by P. Tuohy from Standish O'Grady, *The Coming of Cuculain*, 1919.)

When he was old enough, the boy Setanta went to the court of Conor to be brought up and instructed along with the other sons of princes and chieftains. One afternoon King Conor and his nobles were going to a feast at the fortress of a wealthy smith named Cullan, in Quelgny, where they also meant to spend the night. Setanta was to accompany them, but as the cavalcade set off he was in the midst of a game of hurley with his companions and bade the king go forward. The royal company arrived at their destination as night began to fall. Cullan received them hospitably, and when they had entered he barred the gates of his fortress and let loose outside a huge and ferocious dog which every night guarded the lonely mansion.

But they had forgotten Setanta! In the middle of the feast a terrible sound was heard. It was the tremendous baying of the hound of Cullan, giving tongue as it saw a stranger approach. Soon the noise changed to the howls of a fierce combat, but on rushing to the gates, they saw a young boy and the hound lying dead at his feet. When it flew at him he had seized it by the throat and dashed its life out against the side-posts of the gate. The warriors bore in the lad with rejoicing, but there stood their host, silent and sorrowful over the body of his faithful friend.

"Give me", then said the lad Setanta, "a whelp of that hound, O Cullan, and I will train him to be all to you that his sire was. And until then, give me shield and spear and I will myself guard your house; never hound guarded it better than I will."

And all the company shouted applause at the generous pledge, and on the spot they named the lad Cuchulain, the Hound of Cullan, and by that name he was known until he died.

When he was older, and near the time when he might assume the weapons of manhood, he came before the king. "What do you want?" asked Conor. "To take the arms of manhood," said Cuchulain. "So be it," said the king, and he gave the lad two great spears. But Cuchulain shook them in his hand, and the staves splintered and broke. And so he did with many others, and the chariots in which they set him to drive he broke to pieces with stamping of his foot until at last the king's own chariot of war and his two spears and sword were brought to the lad, and these he could not break, do what he would, so this equipment he retained.

The young Cuchulain was by this time grown so fair and noble a youth that every maid or matron on whom he looked was bewitched by him, and the men of Ulster bade him take a wife of his own. But none were pleasing to him, till at last he saw the lovely maiden Emer, daughter of Forgall, the Lord of Lusca, and he resolved to woo her for his bride. So he bade harness his chariot, and with Laeg, his friend and charioteer, he journeyed to Dūn Forgall.

As he drew near, the maiden was with her companions, teaching them embroidery, for in that art she excelled all women. Emer went to meet Cuchulain and saluted him. But when he urged his love upon her she said: "I may not marry before my sister Fial, who is older than I." "It is not Fial whom I love," said Cuchulain. Then as they were conversing he saw the breast of the maiden over the bosom of her smock, and said to her: "Fair is this plain, the plain of the noble yoke." "None comes to this plain," said she, "who has not slain his hundreds, and thy deeds are still to do."

So Cuchulain then left her, and drove back to Emain Macha.

Next day Cuchulain bethought himself how he could prepare himself for

Cullan's huge and ferocious dog was let out every night to guard his house. Hounds from the Book of Kells (Trinity College, Dublin).

Golden coin of the Remi, a tribe from what is now north-eastern France. Charioteers also appeared on coins minted by the Romans, as a sign of respect for the skill of Celtic warriors.

war and for the deeds of heroism which Emer had demanded of him. Now he had heard of a mighty woman-warrior named Skatha, who dwelt in the Land of Shadows, and who could teach to young heroes who come to her wonderful feats of arms. So Cuchulain went overseas to find her, and when he had passed the Plain of Ill-luck, and escaped the beasts of the Perilous Glen, he came to the Bridge of the Leaps, beyond which was the country of Skatha. Here he found on the hither side many sons of the princes of Ireland who were come to learn feats of war from Skatha, and among them was his friend Ferdia, son of the Firbolg, Daman.

He asked Ferdia how he should pass the Bridge of Leaps, which was very narrow and very high.

"Not one of us has crossed that bridge," said Ferdia, "for there are two feats that Skatha teaches last, and one is the leap across the bridge, and the other the thrust of the Gae Bolg."

But Cuchulain waited till evening, when he had recovered his strength from his long journey, and at the fourth leap he lit fairly on the centre of the bridge, and with one leap more he was across it, and stood before the strong fortress of Skatha, and she wondered at his courage and vigour, and admitted him to be her pupil.

For a year and a day Cuchulain abode with Skatha, and all the feats she had to teach he learned easily, and last of all she taught him the use of the Gae Bolg, and gave him that dreadful weapon, which she had deemed no champion before him good enough to have. And the manner of using the Gae Bolg was that it was thrown with the foot, and if it entered an enemy's body it filled every limb and crevice of him with its barbs.

Now whilst Cuchulain was in the Land of the Shadows, it chanced that Skatha made war on the people of the Princess Aifa, who was the fiercest and strongest of the woman-warriors of the world. When the armies met, Cuchulain and the two sons of Skatha slew six of the mightiest of Aifa's warriors. Then Aifa sent word to Skatha and challenged her to single combat. But

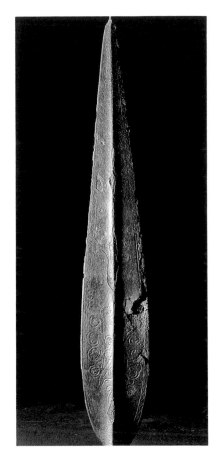

The Gae Bolg, the spear Cuchulain was given by his instructor Skatha, was a kind of barbed harpoon thrown with the feet. (Engraved iron blade of a lance, National Museum, Budapest.)

Cuchulain's son arrives in Ireland in a little boat. This miniature gold boat from Broighter, Co. Derry, was probably an offering to the sea god Mananan. (National Museum of Ireland.)

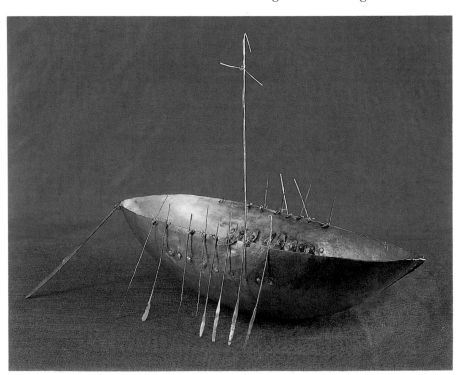

Cuchulain declared that he would go in place of Skatha, and he asked first of all, what were the things Aifa most valued. "What she loves most", said Skatha, "are her two horses, her chariot and her charioteer." Then the pair met in single combat, and at last a blow of Aifa's shattered the sword of Cuchulain to the hilt. At this Cuchulain cried out: "Ah me! behold the chariot and horses of Aifa, fallen into the glen!" Aifa glanced round, and Cuchulain, rushing in, seized her round the waist and slung her over his shoulder and bore her back to the camp of Skatha. She begged for her life, and Cuchulain granted it on condition that she made a lasting peace with Skatha. To this she agreed, and Cuchulain and she became not only friend but lovers.

Before Cuchulain left the Land of Shadows, he gave Aifa a golden ring, saying that if she should bear him a son he was to be sent to seek his father in Erin so soon as he should have grown so that his finger would fit the ring. And Cuchulain said, "Charge him under *geise* that he shall not make himself known, that he never turn out of the way for any man, nor ever refuse a combat. And be his name called Connla."

In later years, when King Conor of Ulster and the lords of Ulster were at a gathering on the Strand of the Footprints, they saw coming towards them, across the sea, a little boat of bronze, and in it a young lad whom none present recognized, with gilded oars in his hands.

When the boy came to land, a messenger, Condery, was sent to bid him be off. "I will not turn back for thee," said the lad. Then Conall of the Victories was sent against him, but the lad slung a great stone at him, knocked him down, and the lad sprang upon him, and bound his arms with the strap of his shield. And so man after man was served. The lad defied the whole power of Ulster to turn him back, nor would he tell his name or lineage.

"Send for Cuchulain," then said King Conor. And they sent a messenger to Dundalk, where Cuchulain was with Emer, his wife, and bade him come to do battle against the strange boy. Emer threw her arm round Cuchulain's neck. "Do not go," she entreated. "Surely this is the son of Aifa. Slay not thine only son." But Cuchulain said: "Forbear, woman! Were it Connla himself I would slay him for the honour of Ulster," and he went to the Strand. Here he found the boy tossing up his weapons and doing marvellous feats with them. "Delightful is your play, boy," said Cuchulain, "who are you and from where do you come?" "I may not reveal that," said the lad. "Then you shall die," said Cuchulain. "So be it," said the lad, and then they fought with swords for a while, but the lad planted himself on a rock and stood so firm that Cuchulain could not move him. At last they both fell into the sea, and Cuchulain was near being drowned, till he bethought himself of the Gae Bolg, and he drove that weapon against the lad and it ripped up his belly. "That is what Skatha never taught me," cried the lad. "Woe is me, for I am hurt." Cuchulain looked at him and saw the ring on his finger. "It is true," he said and he took up the boy and bore him on shore and laid him down before Conor and the lords of Ulster. "Here is my son for you, men of Ulster," he said. This was the only son Cuchulain ever had, and this son he slew. To complete the story of Aifa and her son, we have anticipated events, and now turn back to take up the thread again.

After training under Skatha, Cuchulain returned to Erin, eager to test his prowess and to win Emer for his wife. So he ordered his chariot to be harnessed and drove out to make a foray upon the marches of Connacht, for between Connacht and Ulster there was always fighting along the borders.

The Ulster landscape bears many similarities to that of western Scotland only 25 miles away, where Cuchulain received his training in the Isle of Skye.

And first he drove to the White Cairn, which is on the highest of the Mountains of Mourne, and surveyed the land of Ulster spread out smiling in the sunshine far below. Then turning southwards he looked over the plains of Bregia, and the charioteer pointed out to him Tara and Teltin, and Brugh na Boyna and the great fortress of the sons of Nechtan. "Are they", asked Cuchulain, "those sons of Nechtan of whom it is said that more of the men of Ulster have fallen by their hands than are yet living on the earth?" "The same", said the charioteer. "Then let us drive thither," said Cuchulain. So, much unwilling, the charioteer drove to the fortress of the sons of Nechtan, and there on the green before it they found a pillar-stone, and round it a collar of bronze having on it writing in Ogham. This Cuchulain read, and it declared that any man of age to bear arms who should come to that green should hold it *geis* for him to depart without having challenged one of the dwellers in the fortress to single combat. Then Cuchulain flung his arms round the stone, and, swaying it backwards and forwards, heaved it at last out of the earth and flung it into the river that ran hard by. "Surely", said the charioteer, "you are seeking for a violent death, and now you will find it without delay."

Then Foill, son of Nechtan, came forth from the fortress, and seeing Cuchulain, whom he deemed but a lad, he was annoyed. But Cuchulain bade him fetch his arms, "for I kill neither drivers nor messengers nor unarmed men," and Foill went back into the fortress. "You cannot slay him," then said the charioteer, "for he is invulnerable by magic power to the point or edge of any blade." But Cuchulain put in his sling a ball of tempered iron, and when Foill appeared, he slung at him so that it went clean through his skull, and Cuchulain took his head and bound it to his chariot-rim. And other sons of Nechtan,

A pillar stone with writing in Ogham. Stones bearing inscriptions in Ogham, such as this one at Dromkeare, were often overwritten with Christian symbols later.

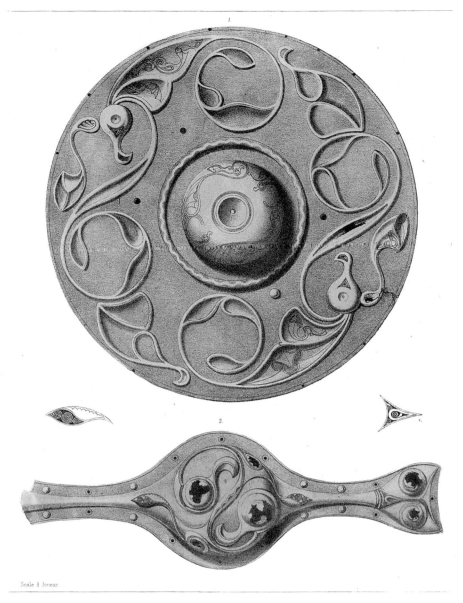

Foill was invulnerable to the point or edge of any blade. Shields with sharpened edges could also be thrown as offensive weapons. Bronze shield mounts. (Illustration from Kemble, Franks and Latham, *Horae Ferales*, 1863.)

issuing forth, he fought with and slew by sword or spear, and then he fired the fortress and drove on exultant. And on the way he saw a flock of wild swans, and sixteen of them he brought down alive with his sling, and tied them to the chariot, and seeing a herd of wild deer he caught two great stags, and with thongs and ropes he made them fast to the chariot.

At Emain Macha, Conor looked to see who was approaching, and he saw that Cuchulain was in his battle-fury, and would deal death around him to anyone he met, so he hastily gave order that a troop of the women of Emania should go forth to meet him, and stand naked in the way. This they did, and when the lad saw them, smitten with shame, he bowed his head upon the chariot-rim. Then Conor's men instantly seized him and plunged him into a vat of cold water until at last his fury left him, and his natural form and aspect were restored. Then they clothed him in fresh raiment and invited him in to the feast in the king's banqueting-hall.

Next day he went to the fortress of Forgall the Wily, father of Emer, and he leaped "the hero's salmon leap", that he had learned of Skatha, over the high ramparts. Then the mighty men of Forgall set on him, and he dealt but three blows, and each blow slew eight men, and Forgall himself fell lifeless in

Cuchulain cut off the head of the demon who immediately rose, took up his head and left. The same story recurs in the medieval tale of the Headless Green Knight in Arthur's Hall (British Library).

leaping from the rampart of the fortress to escape Cuchulain. So he carried off Emer and her foster-sister and two loads of gold and silver. So was Emer won as she desired, and he brought her to Emain Macha and made her his wife, and they were not parted again until he died.

A lord of Ulster named Bricciu of the Poisoned Tongue once made a feast to which he invited King Conor and all the heroes of the Red Branch, and because it was always his delight to stir up strife he set the heroes contending among themselves as to who was the champion of the land of Erin. At last it was agreed that the championship must lie among three of them; namely, Cuchulain, and Conall of the Victories and Laery the Trimphant. To decide between these three a demon named The Terrible was summoned. He proposed to the heroes a test of courage. Any one of them, he said, might cut off his head today provided that he, the claimant of the championship, would lay down his head for the axe to-morrow. Conall and Laery shrank from the test, but Cuchulain accepted it. However, when he cut off the head of the demon, the frightful creature immediately rose, and taking the bleeding head in one hand and his axe in the other, plunged into a lake.

Next day he reappeared, whole and sound, to claim the fulfilment of the bargain. Cuchulain, quailing but resolute, laid his head on the block. The demon swung his axe thrice over his victim, brought down the butt with a crash on the block, and then told Cuchulain to rise unhurt, Champion of Ireland and her boldest man.

DEIRDRE AND THE SONS OF USNA

Deidre and her nurse Levarcam were sent to live in isolation until Deidre was old enough to marry King Conor of Ulster. (Illustration by John D. Batten from Joseph Jacobs, *Celtic Fairy Tales*, 1892.)

Naisi and his brothers bore Deidre away to Scotland, where they lived by fishing and hunting. (Illustration by John D. Batten from Joseph Jacobs, *Celtic Fairy Tales*, 1892.)

There was among the lords of Ulster one named Felim, son of Dall, who on a certain day made a great feast for the king. And the king came with his Druid Cathbad, and Fergus mac Roy, and many heroes of the Red Branch, and while they were making merry, a messenger from the women's apartments came to tell Felim that his wife had just borne him a daughter. So all the lords and warriors drank health to the new-born infant, and the king commanded Cathbad to foretell what the future would have in store for Felim's babe. Cathbad was much troubled, and at length he said: "The infant shall be fairest among the women of Erin, and shall wed a king, but because of her shall death and ruin come upon the Province of Ulster." Then the warriors would have put her to death upon the spot, but Conor forbade them. "I will avert the doom," he said, "for she shall wed no foreign king, but she shall be my own mate when she is of age." So he took away the child, and committed it to his nurse Levarcam, and the name they gave it was Deirdre. And Conor charged Levarcam that the child should be brought up in a strong fortress in the solitude of a great wood until she was of marriageable age.

One day, when the time for the marriage of Deirdre and Conor was drawing near, Deirdre and Levarcam looked over the rampart of their fortress. It was winter, a heavy snow had fallen in the night, and the green before the fortress was a sheet of unbroken white, save that in one place a scullion had killed a calf for their dinner, and the blood of the calf lay on the snow. And as Deirdre looked, a raven lit down from a tree hard by and began to sip the blood. "O nurse", cried Deirdre suddenly, "such, and not like Conor, would be the man that I would love—his hair like the raven's wing, and in his cheek the hue of blood, and his skin as white as snow." "You have pictured Naisi, son of Usna, a champion of the Red Branch," said the nurse. Thereupon Deirdre entreated Levarcam to bring her to speak with Naisi, and because the old woman loved the girl and would not have her wedded to the aged king, she at last agreed. Deirdre implored Naisi to save her from Conor, and he vowed to be hers. Then secretly one night, he came with his two brothers Adran and Ainlé, and bore away Deirdre with Levarcam, and they escaped the king's pursuit, and they made their dwelling in Scotland and there lived in the wild wood by hunting and fishing.

And the years went by and Conor made no sign, but he did not forget, and his spies told him of all that befell Naisi and Deirdre. At last, judging that Naisi and his brothers would have tired of solitude, he sent the bosom friend of Naisi, Fergus, son of Roy, to bid them return, and to promise them that all would be forgiven. Fergus went joyfully, but Deirdre foresaw evil, and would have sent Fergus home alone. Naisi blamed her for her doubt and suspicion, and reminded her that they were under the protection of Fergus, whose safeguard no king in Ireland would dare to violate, and they at last made ready to leave that part of Scotland which had been their home.

On landing in Ireland, they were met by Baruch, a lord of the Red Branch, who had his fortress close by, and he invited Fergus to a feast he had prepared for him that night. "I may not stay," said Fergus, "for I must first convey Deirdre and the sons of Usna safely to Emain Macha." "Nevertheless", said Baruch, "you must stay with me to-night for it is a *geis* to refuse a feast." Deirdre implored him not to leave them, but Fergus feared to break his *geis*, and he bade his two sons, Illan the Fair and Buino the Red, take charge of the party in his place, and he himself stayed with Baruch.

And so the party came to Emain Macha, and they were lodged in the House of the Red Branch, but Conor did not receive them. After the evening meal, as he sat, drinking heavily and silently, he sent a servant named Trendorn to the Red Branch House to mark who was there and what they did. But when Trendorn came, the place was barred for the night, and he mounted on a ladder and looked in at a high window. And there he saw the brothers of Naisi and the sons of Fergus, and Naisi playing chess, and with him the fairest of women that he had ever seen. But as he looked, one caught sight of him. Seizing a chessman from the board, Naisi hurled it at the face of the spy, and it struck out his eye. Then Trendorn hastily descended, and went back with his bloody face to the king. Conor arose, and called for his guards and bade them bring the sons of Usna before him for maiming his messenger. And the guards went, but Buino, with his retinue, met them, and at the sword's point drove them back. Conor went to Buino, and with a great gift of lands he bought him over to desert his charge. Then Illan took up the defence of the Red Branch Hostel, but the two sons of Conor slew him. And then at last Naisi and his brothers seized their weapons and rushed amid the foe, and many were they who fell before the onset. Then Conor entreated Cathbad the Druid to cast spells upon them, and he vowed to do them no hurt if they were taken alive. So Cathbad conjured up, as it were, a lake of slime that seemed to be about the feet of the sons of Usna, and they could not tear their feet from it. Then the guards and servants of Conor seized and bound them and brought them before the king. And the king called upon man after man to come forward and slay the sons of Usna, but none would obey him, till at last Owen, son of Duracht, came and took the sword of Naisi, and with one sweep he cut off the heads of all three, and so they died.

Then Conor took Deirdre by force, and for a year she lived with him in the palace in Emain Macha, but during all that time she never smiled. At length Conor said 'What is it that you hate most of all on earth, Deirdre?" And she said: "You yourself and Owen, son of Duracht," and Owen was standing by. "Then you shall go to Owen for a year," said Conor. But when Deirdre mounted the chariot behind Owen she kept her eyes on the ground, and Conor said, taunting her: "Deirdre, your glance between me and Owen is the glance of a ewe between two rams." Then Deirdre flung herself head foremost from the chariot, dashed her head against a rock and fell dead.

When Fergus mac Roy came home to Emain Macha after the feast to which Baruch invited him, and found the sons of Usna slain and one of his own sons dead and the other a traitor, he vowed to be avenged on Conor with fire and

Pictish carving of bull from Burghead, Inverness. One of the sacred animals of the Celts, the bull also represented the wealth and status of its owner.

sword. And he went off straightway to Connacht to take service of arms with Ailell and Maev, who were king and queen of that country. But though Ailell was king, Maev was the ruler in truth, and ordered all things as she wished, and took what husbands she wished, and dismissed them at pleasure, for she was as fierce and strong as a goddess of war, and knew no law but her own wild will. When Fergus came to her in her palace at Rathcroghan in Roscommon she gave him her love, as she had given it to many before, and they plotted together how to attack and devastate the Province of Ulster.

Fergus went straight to Connacht, to countryside like this at Roundstone, Co. Galway. Supporting the legends, there is evidence of a historical rivalry between Ulster and Connacht around the first century A.D.

THE CATTLE-RAID OF QUELGNY

Now it happened that Maev possessed a famous red bull named Finnbenach, and one day when she and Ailell were counting up their respective possessions and matching them against each other, he taunted her because the Finnbenach had attached himself to Ailell's herd. So Maev in vexation went to her steward, mac Roth, and asked of him if there were anywhere in Erin a bull as fine as the Finnbenach. "Truly", said the steward, "there is—for the Brown Bull of Quelgny, that belongs to Dara, son of Fachtna, is the mightiest beast

Lough Gill, Sligo is in the heart of Connacht and close to Knocknarea Mountain where a huge cairn is traditionally believed to commemorate Queen Maev.

that is in Ireland." And after that Maev felt as if she had no herds that were worth anything at all unless she possessed the Brown Bull of Quelgny. But this was in Ulster, and Maev knew that the Ulstermen would not give up the bull without fighting for it. So she and Fergus and Ailell agreed to make a foray against Ulster for the Brown Bull, for Fergus longed for vengeance, and Maev for fighting, for glory and for the bull, and Ailell to satisfy Maev.

The first attempt of Maev to get possession of the bull was to send an embassy to Dara to ask for the loan of him for a year, the recompense offered being fifty heifers, besides the bull himself back, and if Dara chose to settle in Connacht he should have as much land there as he now possessed in Ulster, and a chariot. Dara sent back a message of refusal and defiance. And so Maev sent messengers around on every side to summon her hosts for the Raid.

And there came all the mighty men of Connacht—first the seven sons of Ailell and Maev, each with his retinue, and Ket and Anluan, sons of Maga, with thirty hundreds of armed men, and yellow-haired Ferdia, with his company of Firbolgs. And there came also the allies of Maev—a host of the men of Leinster, and Cormac, son of Conor, with Fergus mac Roy and other exiles from Ulster, who had revolted against Conor for his treachery to the sons of Usna.

But before the host set forth towards Ulster, Maev sent her spies into the land to tell her of the preparations there being made. And the spies brought back a wondrous tale, and one that rejoiced the heart of Maev, for they said that Macha's curse had descended on the province and there was no hand in Ulster that could lift a spear, except that of Cuchulain, son of Lugh.

On the morrow the host set forth, Fergus mac Roy leading them, and as they neared the confines of Ulster he bade them keep sharp watch, lest Cuchulain of Murthemney, should fall upon them unawares. Now Cuchulain and his father, Sualtam, were on the borders of the province, and Cuchulain, from a warning Fergus had sent him, suspected the approach of a great host, and bade Sualtam go northwards to Emania and warn the men of Ulster. But Cuchulain himself went into the forest, and there, standing on one leg, and using only one hand and one eye, he cut an oak sapling and twisted it into a circular withe. On this he cut in Ogham characters how the withe was made, and he put the host of Maev under *geise* not to pass by that place till one of them had, under similar conditions, made a similar withe, "and I except my friend Fergus mac Roy," he added, and wrote his name at the end. Then he placed the withe round the pillar-stone of Ardcullin, and went his way.

When the host of Maev came to Ardcullin, the withe upon the pillar-stone was found and brought to Fergus to decipher it. There was none amongst the host who could emulate the feat of Cuchulain, and so they went into the wood and encamped for the night.

Cuchulain now followed hard on their track, and as he went, he estimated by the tracks they had left the number of the host at eighteen *triucha cét* (54,000 men). Circling round the host, he now met them in front, and soon came upon two chariots containing scouts sent ahead by Maev. These he slew, each man with his driver, and having with one sweep of his sword cut a forked pole of four prongs from the wood, he drove the pole deep into a river-ford at the place called Athgowla, and impaled on each prong a bloody head. When the

The sight of Cuchulain in his battle frenzy once killed a hundred men. Horned helmets, like this one found in the River Thames, may have been designed to intimidate as well as to protect. (British Museum.)

host came up they wondered and feared at the sight, and Fergus declared that they were under *geise* not to pass that ford till one of them had plucked out the pole even as it was driven in, with the finger-tips of one hand. So Fergus drove into the water and at last he tore it out; as it was now late the host encamped upon the spot. These devices of Cuchulain were intended to delay the invaders until the Ulster men had recovered from their debility.

The host of Maev spread out and devastated the territories of Bregia and of Murthemney, but they could not advance further into Ulster. Cuchulain hovered about them continually, slaying them by twos and threes, and as his wrath grew fiercer, he descended with supernatural might upon whole companies of the Connacht host, and hundreds fell at his onset. At the sight of Cuchulain in his battle-frenzy, it is said that once a hundred of Maev's warriors fell dead from horror.

Maev now tried to tempt him by great largesse to desert the cause of Ulster, but she failed to move him, and death descended more thickly than ever upon the Connacht host. At last, through the mediation of Fergus, an agreement was come to. Cuchulain undertook not to harry the host, provided they would only send against him one champion at a time, whom Cuchulain would meet in

Ferdia and Cuchulain took their heavy swords. On average about one metre in length, Celtic iron swords were intended as cutting rather than stabbing weapons. (Illustration from Kemble, Franks and Latham, *Horae Ferales*, 1863.)

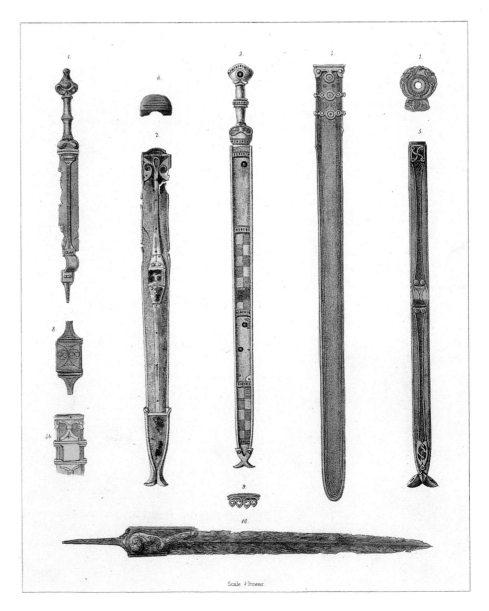

68

battle at the ford of the River Dee. While each fight was in progress the host might move on, but when it was ended they must come to a halt and make camp till the morrow morning. "Better to lose one man a day than a hundred," said Maev, and the pact was made.

Several single combats followed, in which Cuchulain was always victor. Maev even persuaded Fergus to go against him, but Fergus and Cuchulain would on no account fight each other, and Cuchulain, by agreement with Fergus, pretended to fly before him, on Fergus's promise that he would do the same for Cuchulain when required.

During one of Cuchulain's duels with a famous champion, Natchrantal, Maev, with a third of her army, made a sudden foray into Ulster. The Brown Bull had taken refuge with his herd of cows in a glen of Slievegallion, Co. Armagh. The raiders of Maev found him there, and drove him off with the herd in triumph, passing Cuchulain as they returned. Cuchulain slew the leader of the escort but could not rescue the Bull, which was taken out of Ulster.

Ferdia

Although the raid ought to have ceased, Maev continued to send warriors against Cuchulain, and he overcame them all save only the mightiest of them all after Fergus, Ferdia son of Daman. And because Ferdia was the old friend and fellow pupil of Cuchulain, he had never gone out against him. But Maev bade him go, lest the poets and satirists of Erin should make verses on him and put him to open shame, and he consented to go. Then was gloom among all his people, for they knew that if Cuchulain and their master met, one of them would return alive no more.

Very early in the morning Ferdia drove to the Ford, and lay down and slept till Cuchulain should come. Not till it was full daylight did Ferdia's charioteer hear the thunder of Cuchulain's war-car approaching, and then he woke his master, and the two friends faced each other across the Ford. And when they had greeted each other, they debated with what weapons they should begin the fight, and Ferdia reminded Cuchulain of the art of casting small javelins that they had learned from Skatha, and they agreed to begin with these. Backwards and forwards, then, across the Ford, hummed the light javelins, but when noonday had come, not one weapon had pierced the defence of either champion. Then they took to the heavy missile spears, and now at last blood began to flow. At last the day came to its close. "Let us cease now," said Ferdia, and Cuchulain agreed, and the friends embraced and kissed each other three times, and went to their rest.

Next day they betook themselves again to the Ford. Cuchulain chose then the heavy, broad-bladed spears for close fighting, and with them they fought from the chariots till the sun went down, and the body of each hero was torn with wounds. Then at last they kissed each other as before, and slept peacefully till the morning.

When the third day of the combat came, it was the turn of Ferdia to choose the weapons, and they took their heavy swords, and though they cut from each other's thighs and shoulders great cantles of flesh, neither could prevail over the other, and at last night ended the combat. This time they parted from each other in heaviness and gloom.

On the fourth day Ferdia knew the contest would be decided, and he armed himself with especial care.

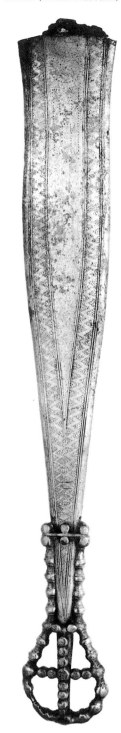

Bronze sheath of the La Tène culture from Richmond. The intricate decorations were evidence of the rank and wealth of the owner. (British Museum.)

Cuchulain seized Ferdia as he fell and carried him across the ford. (Illustration from T. W. H. Rolleston, *Myths of the Celtic Race*, 1911.)

Cuchulain's horse, the Grey of Macha, has a supernatural intelligence which sets it among the creatures of myth. (Illustration from Standish O'Grady, *Finn and his Companions*, 1892.)

"O Ferdia", said Cuchulain when they met, "what shall be our weapons to-day?" "It is your choice today," said Ferdia. "Then let it be all or any," said Cuchulain, and Ferdia was cast down at hearing this, but he said, "So be it," and thereupon the fight began. Till midday they fought with spears, but neither of the two great warriors could gain any advantage over the other.

Then at last Cuchulain's frenzy came upon him, and he dilated giant-like, till he overtopped Ferdia. And now Ferdia found Cuchulain a moment off his guard, and smote him with the edge of the sword, and it sank deep into his flesh. And he pressed Cuchulain sorely after that, so that Cuchulain could endure it no longer, and he shouted to his driver to fling him the Gae Bolg. When Ferdia heard that he lowered his shield to guard himself from below, and Cuchulain drove his spear over the rim of the shield and into his chest. And Ferdia raised his shield again, but in that moment Cuchulain seized the Gae Bolg in his toes and drove it upward against Ferdia, and deep into his body it passed. " 'Tis enough," cried Ferdia, "I have my death of that. It is an ill deed that I fall by thy hand, O Cuchulain." Cuchulain seized him as he fell, and carried him northward across the Ford, that he might die on the further side of it, and not on the side of the men of Erin. And from Ulster came certain of the friends of Cuchulain, and they bore him away into Murthemney, and his kin among the Danaan cast magical herbs into the rivers for his healing. But he lay there in weakness and in stupor for many days.

The Rousing of Ulster

Now Sualtam, the husband of Cuchulain's mother, had taken his son's horse, the Grey of Macha, and ridden off again to see if by any means he might rouse the men of Ulster to defend the province. At last he came to Emania, and there were Cathbad the Druid and Conor the King, and all their nobles and lords, and Sualtam cried aloud to them: "Cuchulain alone holds the gap of Ulster against the four provinces of Erin. Arise and defend yourselves!" But Cathbad only said: "Death were the due of him who thus disturbs the King."

Then Sualtam wheeled round his horse in anger and was about to depart when, with a start which the Grey made, his neck fell against the sharp rim of the shield upon his back, and it shore off his head, and the head fell on the ground. Yet still it cried its message as it lay, and at length into the clouded mind of the king the truth began to penetrate, and slowly the spell of Macha's curse was lifted.

With the curse now departed from them, the men of Ulster flocked joyfully to the summons, and Conor's host fell upon eight score of the men of Erin in Meath and they slew every man. Maev and her host then fell back toward Connacht, but when they reached the Hill of Slane, in Meath, the Ulster bands joined each other there and prepared to give battle.

The battle was joined on the Plain of Garach, in Meath. Fergus, wielding a two-handed sword, swept down whole ranks of the Ulster men at each blow, and the fierce Maev charged thrice into the heart of the enemy.

Fergus met Conor the King and smote him on his shield, but Cormac, the king's son, begged for his father's life. Fergus then turned on Conall of the Victories, one of the heroes of Ulster.

"Too hot are you," said Conall, "against your people for a wanton." Fergus then turned from slaying the Ulstermen, but in his battle-fury he smote among

the hills with his rainbow-sword, and struck off the tops of the three *Maela* of Meath, so that they are flat-topped to this day.

Cuchulain in his stupor heard the crash of Fergus's blows, and coming slowly to himself he asked of Laeg what it meant. "It is the sword-play of Fergus," said Laeg. Then he sprang up, armed himself, and rushed into the battle. Here he met Fergus. "Turn hither, Fergus," he shouted, "avoid me as you are pledged."

"I have promised even that," said Fergus, and then went out of the battle, and with him the men of Leinster and the men of Munster, leaving Maev with her seven sons and the hosting of Connacht alone.

It was midday when Cuchulain came into the fight; when the evening sun was shining through the trees his war-chariot was but two wheels and a handful of shattered ribs, and the host of Connacht was in full flight towards the border. Cuchulain overtook Maev, who crouched under her chariot and entreated grace. "I am not wont to slay women," said Cuchulain, and he protected her till she had crossed the Shannon at Athlone.

The Brown Bull of Quelgny that Maev had sent into Connacht by a circuitous way, met the white-horned Bull of Ailell on the Plain of Aei, and the two beasts fought, but the Brown Bull quickly slew the other, and tossed his fragments about the land, and then careered madly about till he fell dead, bellowing and vomiting black gore, at the Ridge of the Bull, between Ulster and Iveagh. Ailell and Maev made peace with Ulster for seven years, and the Ulster men returned home to Emain Macha with great glory.

The Vengeance of Maev

Though Maev made peace with Ulster after the battle of Garech, she vowed the death of Cuchulain for all the shame and loss he had brought upon her and on her province since she first set her heart on acquiring the Brown Bull.

All those who bore a grudge against Cuchulain now did Maev rouse by secret messages, and they waited till they heard that the curse of Macha was again heavy on the men of Ulster, and then they assembled a host and

The battle was joined. In this panel from the Gundestrup cauldron, mounted warriors and foot soldiers are depicted apparently marching to war. (National Museum of Denmark.)

The Brown Bull of Quelgny and the Bull of Ailell met and fought, and the Brown Bull slew the other. (Illustration by Joan Kiddell-Monroe.)

marched to the Plain of Murthemney. And first the Children of Calatin the wizard, whom Cuchulain had slain, made the semblance of armed battalions marching against Murthemney, and Cuchulain seemed to see on every side the smoke of burning dwellings going up. And for two days he did battle with the phantoms till he was sick and wearied out. Then Cathbad and the men of Ulster persuaded him to retire to a solitary glen, where fifty of the princess of Ulster, and among them Niam, wife of his faithful friend Conall of the Victories, tended him, and Niam made him vow that he would not leave the fortress where he was, until she gave him leave.

But still the Children of Calatin filled the land with apparitions of war, and smoke and flames went up, and wild cries and wailings with chattering, goblin laughter, and the braying of trumpets and horns were borne upon the winds. And Bave, Calatin's daughter, went into the glen, and, taking the form of a handmaid of Niam, she beckoned her away and put a spell of straying on her so that she could find her way home no more. Bave then went in the form of Niam to Cuchulain and bade him up and rescue Ulster from the hosts that were harrying it, and the Morrigan came in the form of a great crow and croaked of war and slaughter.

Then Cuchulain, having armed himself, drove forth, and on every side shapes and sounds of dread assailed him, and it appeared to him that he saw a great smoke over the ramparts of Emain Macha, and he thought he saw the corpse of Emer tossed out over the ramparts. But when he came to his fortress at Murthemney, there was Emer living, and she entreated him to leave the phantoms alone, but he would not listen to her. Then he bade farewell to his mother Dectera, and she gave him a goblet of wine to drink, but before he could drink it the wine turned to blood, and he flung it away, saying, "My life's end is near; this time I shall not return alive from the battle." And Dectera and Cathbad besought him to await the coming of Conall of the Victories, who was away on a journey, but he would not.

Near to Slieve Fuad, south of Armagh, Cuchulain found the host of his enemies, and drove furiously against them until the plain was strewn with their dead. Then a satirist, urged on by Lewy, came near him and demanded his spear. "Have it, then," said Cuchulain, and flung it at him with such force that it not only went clean through him but killed another nine men beyond.

Then another satirist demanded the spear, and Cuchulain said: "I am not bound to grant more than one request on one day." But the satirist said: "Then I will revile Ulster for your default," and Cuchulain flung him the spear. Erc now got it, and this time in flying back it struck the Grey of Macha. Cuchulain drew out the spear from the horse's side, and the Grey galloped away.

And a third time Cuchulain flung the spear to a satirist, and Lewy took it again and flung it back, and it struck Cuchulain, and his bowels fell out in the chariot, and the remaining horse, Black Sainglend, broke away and left him.

"I would go as far as to that loch-side to drink," said Cuchulain, knowing the end was come, and they suffered him to go when he had promised to return to them again. So he gathered up his bowels into his breast and went to the loch-side, and drank, and bathed himself, and came forth again to die. And the host gathered round, but feared to approach him while the life was still in him, and the hero-light shone above his brow.

And then came a crow and settled on his shoulder. Lewy, when he saw this, drew near and with his sword he smote off his head; and the sword fell from Cuchulain's hand, and smote off the hand of Lewy as it fell. They took the hand of Cuchulain in revenge for this, and bore the head and hand south to Tara, and there buried them, and over them they raised a mound. But Conall of the Victories met the Grey of Macha streaming with blood, and together they went to the loch-side and saw Cuchulain's body. Conall drove southwards and he came on Lewy by the river Liffey, and slew him, and took his head, and returned to Emain Macha. But they made no show of triumph in entering the city, for Cuchulain the Hound of Ulster was no more.

The death of Cuchulain. "The host feared to approach him while the hero-light shone above his brow." (Illustration from Standish O'Grady, *The Triumph and Passing of Cuchulain.*)

Dectera gave him a goblet of wine. The silver Ardagh chalice, only 18 cm high, is decorated with coloured enamels and gold wire. (National Museum of Ireland.)

CHAPTER V

TALES OF THE OSSIANIC CYCLE

As the tales of the Ultonian Cycle cluster round the heroic figure of the Hound of Cullan, so do those of the Ossianic Cycle round that of Finn mac Cumhal, whose son Oisīn (or Ossian) was a poet as well as a warrior, and is the traditional author of most of them. The events of the Ultonian Cycle are supposed to have taken place about the time of the birth of Christ. Those of the Ossianic Cycle fell mostly in the reign of Cormac mac Art, who lived in the third century A.D. During his reign the Fianna of Erin, who are represented as a kind of military Order composed mainly of the members of two clans, Clan Bascna and Clan Morna, and who were supposed to be devoted to the service of the High King and to the repelling of foreign invaders, reached the height of their renown under the captaincy of Finn.

THE ADVENTURES OF FINN

Finn, like most of the Irish heroes, had a partly Danaan ancestry. His mother, Murna of the White Neck, was grand-daughter of Nuada of the Silver Hand. Cumhal, son of Trenmōlr, was Finn's father. He was chief of the Clan Bascna, who were contending with the Clan Morna for the leadership of the Fianna, and was overthrown and slain by these at the battle of Knock.

Murna, after the defeat and death of Cumhal, took refuge in the forests of Slieve Bloom, and there she bore a child whom she named Demna. For fear that the Clan Morna would find him out and slay him, she gave him to be nurtured in the wildwood by two aged women, and she herself became wife to the King of Kerry. But Demna, when he grew up to be a lad, was called "Finn", or the Fair One, on account of the whiteness of his skin and his golden hair, and by this name he was always known thereafter. His first deed was to slay Lia, who had the Treasure Bag of the Fianna, which he took from him. He then sought out his uncle Crimmal, who, with a few other old men, survivors of the chiefs of Clan Bascna, had escaped the sword at Castleknock, and were living in much penury in the forests of Connacht. These he furnished with a

Moone High Cross, Co. Kildare. This ancient Celtic cross stands over 5 metres high and is carved with 51 panels of Biblical scenes.

The arrival of Christianity meant that Celtic deities like Cernunnos (opposite), the stag god, were transformed into images of devils. Stained-glass window from Fairford in Gloucestershire.

In the River Boyne lived Fintan, the Salmon of Knowledge, "which whoso ate of him would enjoy all the wisdom of the ages". (Illustration by Arthur Rackham from James Stephens, *Irish Fairy Tales*, 1920.)

retinue and guard from among a body of youths who followed his fortunes, and gave them the Treasure Bag. He himself went to learn poetry and science from an ancient Druid named Finegas, who dwelt on the river Boyne. Here, in a pool of this river, under boughs of hazel from which dropped the Nuts of Knowledge on the stream, lived Fintan the Salmon of Knowledge, which whoso ate of him would enjoy all the wisdom of the ages. Finegas had sought many a time to catch this salmon, but failed until Finn had come to be his pupil. Then one day he caught it, and gave it to Finn to cook, bidding him eat none of it himself, but to tell him when it was ready. When the lad brought the salmon, Finegas saw that his countenance was changed. "Have you eaten of the salmon?" he asked. "Nay," said Finn, "but when I turned it on the spit my thumb was burnt, and I put it to my mouth in order to lessen the pain." "Take the Salmon of Knowledge and eat it," then said Finegas, "for in you the prophecy is come true. And now go, for I can teach you no more."

After that Finn became as wise as he was strong and bold, and it is said that whenever he wished to divine what would befall, or what was happening at a distance, he had only to put his thumb in his mouth and bite it, and the knowledge he wished for would be his.

At this time Goll, son of Morna, was the captain of the Fianna of Erin, but Finn, being come to man's estate, wished to take the place of his father Cumhal. So he went to Tara, and during the Great Assembly, sat down among the king's warriors and the Fianna. The king accepted him gladly, and Finn swore loyal service to him. Not long after that came the period of the year when Tara was troubled by a goblin or demon that came at nightfall and blew fire-balls against the royal city, setting it in flames, and none could do battle with him, for as he came he played on a harp a music so sweet that each man who heard it was lapped in dreams, and forgot all else on earth. When this was told to Finn, he went to the king and said: "Shall I, if I slay the goblin, have my father's place as captain of the Fianna?" "Yea, surely," said the king, and he bound himself to this by an oath.

Now there was among the men-at-arms an old follower of Finn's father, Cumhal, who possessed a magic spear, and it had the property that when the naked blade was laid against the forehead of a man, it would fill him with a strength and a battle-fury that would make him invincible in every combat. This spear the man Fiacha gave to Finn, and taught him how to use it, and with it he awaited the coming of the goblin on the ramparts of Tara. As night fell and mists began to gather in the wide plain around the Hill, he saw a shadowy form coming swiftly towards him, and heard the notes of the magic harp. But having the spear to his brow, he shook off the spell, and the phantom fled, and Finn overtook and slew him, and bore back his head to Tara.

Then Cormac the King set Finn before the Fianna, and bade them all either swear obdience to him as their captain or seek service elsewhere.

Finn's Chief Men

With the coming of Finn, the Fianna of Erin came to their glory, and with his life their glory passed away. Thus it is told that Conan, son of the lord of Luachar, him who had the Treasure Bag and whom Finn slew at Rath Luachar, was for seven years an outlaw and marauder, harrying the Fians. At last they ran him into a corner at Carn Lewy, in Munster, and when he saw that he could escape no more, he stole upon Finn as he sat down after a chase, and flung his arms round him from behind, holding him fast and motionless. Finn knew who held him thus, and said: "What do you wish, Conan?" Conan said. "To make a covenant of service and fealty with you, for I may no longer evade your wrath." So Finn laughed and said: "Be it so, Conan, and if you prove faithful and valiant I also will keep faith." Conan served him for thirty years, and no man of all the Fianna was keener and hardier in fight.

There was also another Conan; namely, mac Morna, whose tongue was bitter and scurrilous; no high or brave thing was done that Conan the Bald did not mock and belittle. It is said that when he was stripped, he showed down his back and buttocks a black sheep's fleece instead of a man's skin, and this is

Finn heard the notes of the magic harp but shook off the spell. (Illustration by Stephen Reid from T. W. H. Rolleston, *The High Deeds of Finn*, 1910.)

the way it came about. One day when Conan and certain others of the Fianna were hunting in the forest they came to a stately fortress, but within they found no man, but a great empty hall and a table set forth with a sumptuous feast. So they set themselves gaily to eat and drink, but one of them started to his feet with a cry of fear and wonder, and they all looked round, and saw before their eyes the tapestried walls changing to rough wooden beams, and the ceiling to foul sooty thatch like that of a herdman's hut. So they all sprang to their feet and made for the doorway, all but Conan the Bald, who was gluttonously devouring the good things on the table, and heeded nothing else. Then they shouted to him, and he strove to rise and follow, but found himself limed to the chair so that he could not stir. So two of the Fianna rushed back and seized his arms, and as they dragged him away, they left the most part of his raiment and his skin sticking to the chair. Then, not knowing what else to do with him in his sore plight, they clapped upon his back the nearest thing they could find, which was the skin of a black sheep that they took from a peasant's flock hard by, and it grew there, and Conan wore it till his death.

Another good man that Finn had was Geena, the son of Luga. When his time to take arms was come, he stood before Finn and made his covenant of fealty, and Finn gave him the captaincy of a band. But mac Luga proved slothful and selfish, and at last the Fians under him came with their whole company

The Fianna (below and opposite) were a band of elite fighting men of the third century. These two warriors from the Book of Kells belong to a pagan tradition, but have been incorporated into the Gospels by Christian scribes.

to Finn and laid their complaint against mac Luga, and said: "Choose now, O Finn, whether you will have us or the son of Luga by himself."

Then Finn sent to mac Luga and questioned him, but mac Luga could say nothing to the point as to why the Fianna would none of him. Then Finn taught him the things befitting a youth of noble birth and a captain of men.

In the time of Finn no one was ever permitted to be one of the Fianna of Erin unless he could pass through many severe tests of his worthiness. He must be versed in the Twelve Books of Poetry, and must himself be skilled to make verse in the rime and metre of the masters of Gaelic poesy. Then he was buried to his middle in the earth, and must, with a shield and a hazel stick, there defend himself against nine warriors casting spears at him, and if he were wounded he was not accepted. Then his hair was woven into braids, and he was chased through the forest by the Fians. If he were overtaken, or if a braid of his hair were disturbed, or if a dry stick cracked under his foot, he was not accepted. He must be able to leap over a lath level with his brow, and to run at full speed under one level with his knee, and he must be able while running to draw out a thorn from his foot and never slacken speed. He must take no dowry with a wife.

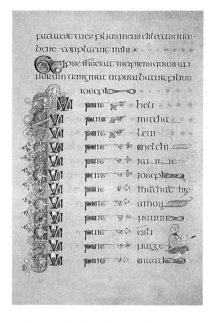

Finn and his hounds (below) pursue a beautiful fawn on the Hill of Allen. (Illustration by Arthur Rackham from James Stephens, *Irish Fairy Tales*, 1920.)

Oisīn

One day, as Finn and his companions and dogs were returning from the chase to their fortress on the Hill of Allen, a beautiful fawn started up on their path, and the chase swept after her. Soon all the pursuers were left far behind, save only Finn himself and his two hounds Bran and Skolawn.

At last, as the chase went on down a valley-side, Finn saw the fawn stop and lie down, while the two hounds began to play round her, and lick her face and limbs. So he gave commandment that none should hurt her, and she followed them to the Fortress of Allen, playing with the hounds as she went.

The same night, Finn awoke and saw standing by his bed the fairest woman his eyes had ever beheld.

"I am Saba, O Finn," she said, "and I was the fawn you chased today. Because I would not give my love to the Druid of the Fairy Folk, he put that shape upon me and I have borne it these three years. But a slave of his, pitying me, once revealed to me that if I could win to the Dūn of Allen, I should be safe from all enchantments, and my natural shape would come to me again."

So Saba dwelt with Finn, and he made her his wife, and so deep was his love for her that neither the battle nor the chase had any delight for him, and for months he never left her side. But at last word came to Finn that the warships of the Northmen were in the Bay of Dublin, and he summoned his heroes to the fight.

Seven days was Finn absent, and he drove the Northmen from the shores of Erin. But on the eighth day he returned, and when he entered his fortress he saw trouble in the eyes of his men and Saba was not on the rampart expecting his return. So he bade them tell him what had chanced, and they said:

"Whilst you were afar off smiting the foreigner we saw one day, as it were, the likeness of you approaching, and Bran and Skolawn at your heels. Then Saba hastened to the great gate, but when she came near she halted and gave a loud cry, and the phantom smote her with a hazel wand, and lo, there was no woman there any more, but only a deer. Then those hounds chased it, and no matter how it strove to reach again the gate of the dūn they turned it back.

Ben Bulben in Sligo. This impressive
outcrop was reputedly the favourite
hunting ground of Finn. From Beltain to
Samhain (April to October), the Fianna
hunted and lived like nomads.

Finn called his name Oisin. Through his
mother Saba, Oisin has been identified
with the Celtic stag god Cernunnos,
portrayed here on the Gundestrup
cauldron. (National Museum of
Denmark.)

What we could do, O Finn, we did; despite our efforts, Saba is gone."

Finn then struck his hand on his breast, but spoke no word, and he went to
his own chamber. Then he came forth, and ordered the matters of the Fianna
as of old, but for seven years thereafter he went searching for Saba through
every remote glen and dark forest of Ireland, and he would take no hounds
with him save Bran and Skolawn. But at last he renounced all hope of finding
her again, and went hunting as of old. One day as he was following the chase
on Ben Bulben, in Sligo, he heard the bay of the dogs change to a fierce growl-
ing, and running hastily up he and his men beheld, under a great tree, a naked
boy with long hair, and around him the hounds struggling to seize him, but
Bran and Skolawn fighting with them and keeping them off. The Fians beat off
the dogs and brought the lad home with them. In time, the use of speech came
to him, and the story that he told was this:

He had known no father and no mother, save a gentle hind, with whom he
lived in a most green and pleasant valley shut in on every side by towering cliffs

that could not be scaled or by deep chasms in the earth. And there came to them sometimes a tall, dark-visaged man, who spoke to his mother, now tenderly, and now in loud menace, but she always shrank away in fear, and the man departed in anger. Then at length the dark man drew near and smote her with a hazel wand, and with that he turned and went his way, but she this time followed him, still looking back at her son and piteously complaining. And he found himself unable to move a limb, and crying out with rage and desolation, he fell to the earth, and his senses left him. When he came to himself he was on the mountain-side on Ben Bulben, and after a while the dogs found him, but of the hind his mother and of the Dark Druid there is no man knows the end.

Finn called his name Oisín (Little Fawn), and he became a warrior of fame, but far more famous for the songs and tales that he made.

It happened that on a misty summer morning as Finn and Oisín with many companions were hunting on the shores of Loch Lena, they saw coming towards them a maiden, beautiful exceedingly, riding on a snow-white steed.

"My name", she said, "is Niam of the Golden Hair. I am the daughter of the King of the Land of Youth, and that which has brought me here is the love of thy son Oisín." Then she turned to Oisín, and she spoke to him in the voice of one who has never asked anything but it was granted to her.

"Wilt thou go with me, Oisín, to my father's land?"

And Oisin said: "That will I, and to the world's end," for the fairy spell had so wrought upon his heart that he cared no more for any earthly thing but to have the love of Niam of the Head of Gold.

Then the maiden spoke of the Land Oversea to which she had summoned her lover, and as she spoke, a dreamy stillness fell on all things till she had made an end.

On a misty summer morning Finn and Oisin saw a beautiful maiden riding towards them. The lakes of Killarney grouped around Lough Leane offer some of the most romantic scenery in Ireland.

As the magic song ended, the Fians beheld Oisīn mount the fairy steed and hold the maiden in his arms, and the young couple fled, as a beam of light flies over the land when clouds drive across the sun and never did the Fianna behold Oisīn son of Finn on earth again after this time.

When the white horse with its riders reached the sea, it ran lightly over the waves, and into a golden haze in which Oisīn lost all knowledge of where he was. But strange sights sometimes appeared to them in the mist, for towers and palace gateways loomed up and disappeared, and once a hornless doe bounded by them, chased by a white hound with one red ear; and again they saw a young maid ride by on a brown steed, bearing a golden apple in her hand, and close behind her followed a young horseman on a white steed, a purple cloak floating at his back and a gold-hilted sword in his hand. And Oisīn would have asked the princess who and what these apparitions were, but Niam bade him ask nothing until they were come to the Land of Youth.

Oisīn met with various adventures in the Land of Youth, but at last, after what seemed to him a sojourn of three weeks in the Land of Youth, he was satiated with delights of every kind, and longed to visit his native land again and to see his old comrades. He promised to return when he had done so, and Niam gave him the steed that had borne him across the sea to Fairyland, but charged him that when he had reached the Land of Erin again he must never alight from its back or the way of return to the Land of Youth would be barred to him for ever. Oisīn then set forth, and found himself at last on the western shores of Ireland. Here he made at once for the Hill of Allen, where the dūn of Finn was wont to be, but he only saw grassy mounds overgrown with rank weeds and whin bushes. Then a strange horror fell upon him and he rode in terror from that place, setting his face towards the eastern sea, for he meant to

Oisin and Niam saw towers and palaces on their journey to the Land of Youth. (Illustration by Stephen Reid from T. W. H. Rolleston, *The High Deeds of Finn*, 1910.)

Oisin made for the Hill of Allen but found only grassy mounds. Before nineteenth-century Englishmen destroyed many of them, the Hill of Tara was covered in mounds and forts marking previous occupation.

The Brown's Hill dolmen has a capstone weighing 100 tons and is thought to be the largest prehistoric marker of its kind in Ireland.

Oisin stopped to help move a great boulder. Nobody is sure how the builders of megalithic monuments raised such huge stones. (Illustration from Francis Grose, *The Antiquities of Ireland*, 1791.)

traverse Ireland from side to side and end to end in the hope that he would be able to find some escape from his enchantment.

But when he came near to the eastern sea, he saw in a field upon the hillside a crowd of men striving to roll aside a great boulder from their tilled land, and an overseer directing them. As he came near they all stopped their work to gaze upon him, for to them he appeared like a messenger of the Fairy Folk. And as Oisīn looked upon their puny forms, he was filled with pity, and stooped from his saddle to help them. He set his hand to the boulder, and with a mighty heave he lifted it from where it lay and set it rolling down the hill. But his saddle-girth burst as he heaved the stone and he fell headlong to the ground. In an instant the white steed had vanished, and that which rose, feeble and staggering, from the ground was no youthful warrior, but a man stricken with extreme old age, white-bearded and withered, who stretched out groping hands and moaned with feeble cries.

When the people saw that the doom that had been wrought was not for them they returned, and found the old man prone on the ground with his face hidden in his arms. So they lifted him up, and asked who he was and what had befallen him. Oisīn gazed round on them with dim eyes, and at last said: "I was Oisīn, the son of Finn." Then the overseer said: "Thou art daft, old man. Finn, son of Cumhal and all his generation have been dead these three hundred years."

TALES OF DERMOT

A number of curious legends centre on Dermot O'Dyna, one of Finn mac Cumhal's most notable followers. He might be described as a kind of Gaelic Adonis. Dermot's father, Donn, gave the child to be nurtured by Angus Ōg, son of the Dagda, in his palace on the Boyne. His mother, who was unfaithful to Donn, bore another child to Roc, the steward of Angus. Donn, one day, when the steward's child ran between his knees to escape from some hounds

The boar roamed the forests of Ben Bulben.
Although he was foster-son of Aengus
Og, Dermot could not avoid being killed
by the boar.

that were fighting on the floor of the hall, gave him a squeeze with his two knees that killed him on the spot, and he then flung the body among the hounds on the floor. When the steward found his son dead, and discovered the cause of it, he brought a Druid rod and smote the body with it, whereupon, in place of the dead child, there arose a huge boar, without ears or tail, and to it he said: "I charge you to bring Dermot O'Dyna to his death," and the boar rushed out from the hall and roamed in the forests of Ben Bulben in Co. Sligo till the time when his destiny should be fulfilled.

But Dermot grew up into a splendid youth, tireless in the chase, undaunted in war, beloved by all his comrades of the Fianna, whom he joined as soon as he was of age to do so.

With three comrades, Goll, Conan and Oscar, Dermot was hunting one day, and late at night they sought a resting-place. They soon found a hut, in which were an old man, a young girl, a sheep and a cat. Here they asked for hospitality, and it was granted to them. But it was a house of mystery.

When they sat down to dinner, the sheep got up and mounted on the table. One after another the Fianna strove too throw it off, but it shook them down on the floor. At last Goll succeeded in flinging it off the table, but him too it vanquished in the end, and put them all under its feet. Then the old man bade the cat lead the sheep back and fasten it up, and it did so easily. The four champions, overcome with shame, were for leaving the house at once but the old man explained that they had suffered no discredit—the sheep they had been fighting with was the World, and the cat was the power that would destroy the world itself; namely, Death.

At night the four heroes went to rest in a large chamber, and the young maid came to sleep in the same room. One after another the Fianna went over to her couch, but she repelled them all. "I belonged to you once," she said to each, "and I never will again." Last of all Dermot went. "O Dermot," she said, "you, also, I belonged to once, and I never can again, for I am Youth, but come here and I will put a mark on you so that no woman can ever see you without loving you." Then she touched his forehead, and left the Love Spot there, and that drew the love of women to him as long as he lived.

The Chase of the Gilla Dacar is another Fian tale in which Dermot plays a leading part. The Fianna, the story goes, were hunting one day on the hills and through the woods of Munster, when they saw coming towards them a huge churl dragging along by a halter a great raw-boned mare. He announced himself as wishful to take service with Finn. The name he was called by, he said, was the Gilla Dacar (the Hard Gilly), because he was the hardest servant ever a lord had to get service or obedience from. In spite of this unpromising beginning, Finn took him into service, and the Fianna now began to make their uncouth comrade the butt of all sorts of rough jokes, which ended in thirteen of them, including Conan the Bald, all mounting up on the Gilla Dacar's steed. On this, the newcomer complained that he was being mocked, and he shambled away in great discontent till he was over the ridge of the hill, when he tucked up his skirts and ran westwards toward the sea-shore in Co. Kerry. Thereupon at once the steed suddenly threw up its head and started off in a furious gallop after its master. The Fianna ran alongside, as well as they could for laughter, while Conan, in terror and rage, reviled them for not rescuing him and his comrades. At last the thing became serious. The Gilla Dacar plunged into the sea, and the mare followed him with her thirteen riders, and one more who managed to cling to her tail just as she left the shore, and all of them soon disappeared towards the fabled region of the West.

Finn and the remaining Fianna decided to fit out a ship and go in search of their comrades. After many days of voyaging, they reached an island guarded by precipitous cliffs. Dermot O'Dyna, as the most agile of the party, was sent to climb them and to discover, if he could, some means of helping up the rest of the party. When he arrived at the top, he found himself in a delightful land, full of the song of birds and the humming of bees and the murmur of streams, but with no sign of habitation. Going into a dark forest, he soon came to a well, by which hung a curiously wrought drinking-horn. As he filled it to drink, a low murmur came from the well, but his thirst was keen and he drank his fill. In no long time there came through the wood an armed warrior, who violently upbraided him for drinking from his well. The Knight of the Well and Dermot then fought all the afternoon without either of them prevailing over the other, when, as evening drew on, the knight suddenly leaped into the well and disappeared. Next day the same thing happened; on the third, however, Dermot, as the knight was about to take his leap, flung his arms round him and would

They reached an island guarded by cliffs. The Minaun Cliffs on Achill, the largest island off the Irish coast. (Illustration by Stephen Gwyn.)

Dermot filled the drinking horn and provoked the anger of the Knight of the Well. (Illustration by Stephen Reid from T. W. H. Rolleston, *The High Deeds of Finn,* 1910.)

not let go, and both of them went down into the well together.

Dermot found himself in Fairyland. A man of noble appearance roused him and led him away to the castle of a great king, where he was hospitably entertained. It was explained to him that the services of a champion like himself were needed to do combat against a rival monarch. Finn and his companions, finding that Dermot did not return to them, found their way up the cliffs, and, having traversed the forest, entered a great cavern which ultimately led them out to the same land as that in which Dermot had arrived. There too, were the fourteen Fianna who had been carried off on the mare of the Hard Gilly. He of course, was the king who needed their services. Finn and his men went into the battle with the best of goodwill, and scattered the enemy like chaff.

Grania and Dermot

Grania was the daughter of Cormac mac Art, High King of Ireland. She was betrothed to Finn mac Cumhal, now an old and war-worn but still mighty warrior. The famous captains of the Fianna all assembled at Tara for the wedding feast, and as they sat at meat Grania surveyed them and asked their names of her father's Druid, Dara. "Who is that man with the spot on his brow?" "That is Dermot O'Dyna," replied the Druid, "in all the world the best

Bronze diadems and collars. Bronze was worked with as much refinement and delicacy as more precious metals. (Illustration from Kemble, Franks and Latham, *Horae Ferales*, 1863.)

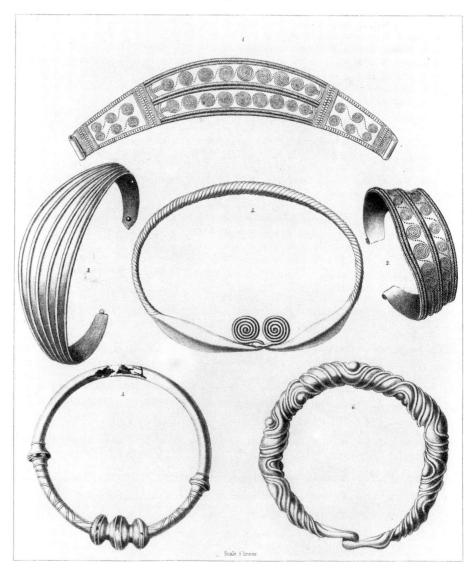

A god from the Gundestrup cauldron, first century B.C., demonstrates his power by holding up men who themselves hold boars (National Museum of Denmark).

lover of women and maidens." Grania now prepared a sleepy draught, which she passed round to the king, to Finn, and to all the company except the chiefs of the Fianna. When the draught had done its work she said, "I put you under *geise*, O Dermot, that you take me out of Tara tonight." And she went off to make ready for the elopement. Dermot, in great perplexity, appealed to Oisín, Oscar, Keelta and the others as to what he should do. They all bade him keep his *geise* and he took leave of them with tears and made his way with Grania to the Ford of Luan on the Shannon.

The Pursuit

Next day Finn, burning with rage, set out with his warriors on their track. He traced out each of their halting-places, and at each place he found a piece of unbroken bread or uncooked salmon—Dermot's subtle message to Finn that he had treated Grania as a sister. But this delicacy of Dermot's was not at all to Grania's mind. They were passing through a piece of wet ground when a splash of water struck Grania. She turned to her companion: "You are a mighty warrior, O Dermot, in battle and sieges and forays, yet meseems that this drop of water is bolder than you." This hint that he was keeping at too respectful a distance was taken by Dermot. The die was now cast, and he would never again meet Finn and his old comrades except at the point of the spear, for Finn was set on vengeance.

Angus Og and his company of the People of Dana were said to live at New Grange, where stones carved with spirals, lozenges and chevrons suggest worship of a mother goddess.

St. Patrick is widely credited with converting the Irish, although by the time he arrived near Downpatrick there were already a number of Christians in the island.

After sixteen years of outlawry, peace was at last made for Dermot by the mediation of Angus with King Cormac and with Finn. Dermot received his proper partimony, and Cormac gave another of his daughters to Finn. Grania bore to Dermot four sons and a daughter.

But Grania was not satisfied until the two best men that were in Erin, namely, Cormac, son of Art, and Finn, son of Cumhal, had been entertained in her house. The King and Finn accepted the invitation, and they and their retinues were feasted for a year at Rath Grania.

Then one night, towards the end of the year of feasting, Dermot was awakened from sleep by the baying of a hound, and on the morrow he went forth armed with sword and sling, and followed by his own hound, to see what was afoot.

On the mountain of Ben Bulben, in Sligo, he came across Finn with a hunting party of the Fianna. They had roused up the enchanted boar without ears or tail, the

Boar of Ben Bulben, which had slain thirty of them that morning. "Come away," said Finn, "for you are under *geise* not to hunt pig." "How is that?" said Dermot, and Finn then told him the story of the death of the steward's son, Dermot's half-brother, and his revivification in the form of this boar, with its mission of vengeance. "By my word," said Dermot, "it is to slay me that you have made this hunt, O Finn, and if it be here that I am fated to die, I have no power now to shun it."

The beast then appeared on the face of the mountain, and Dermot struck him with his sword, but the weapon flew in two and not a bristle of the boar was cut. In the charge of the boar Dermot fell over him, and was carried for a space clinging to his back, but at last the boar shook him off and ripped out his bowels, while at the same time, with the hilt of the sword still in his hand, Dermot dashed out the brains of the beast, and it fell dead beside him.

The implacable Finn then came up, and stood over Dermot in his agony. Dermot begged him to heal him with a draught of water from his hands, for Finn had the magic gift of restoring any wounded man to health with a draught of well-water drawn in his two hands. But Dermot died before the healing draught could reach his lips. When the people of Grania's household went out to fetch in the body of Dermot they found there Angus Ōg and his company of the People of Dana, who, after raising three bitter and terrible cries, bore away the body on a gilded bier.

The Lia Fail or Stone of Destiny at Tara, site of St Patrick's contest of miracles with the Druids. The stone was said to cry out when sat upon by a king.

Patrick's most effective confrontation with the pagans took place at Tara, where he lit a Paschal fire on the Hill of Slane in defiance of the king. (Illustration from Standish O'Grady, *Finn and his Companions*, 1892.)

END OF THE FIANNA

After the death of Cormac mac Art, his son of Cairbry came to the High-Kingship of Ireland. He had a fair daughter named *Sgeimh Solais* (Light of Beauty), who was asked in marriage by a son of the King of the Decies. The marriage was arranged, and the Fianna claimed a ransom or tribute of twenty ingots of gold. It would seem that the Fianna had now grown to be a distinct power within the State, exacting heavy tributes all over Ireland. Cairbry resolved to break them; and he thought he had now a good opportunity to do so. He therefore refused payment of the ransom, and summoned all the provincial kings to help him against the Fianna, the main body of whom immediately went into rebellion for what they deemed their rights. The old feud between Clan Bascna and Clan Morna now broke out afresh, the latter standing by the High King, while Clan Bascna, aided by the King of Munster and his forces, who alone took their side, marched against Cairbry. The decisive battle of the war which ensued took place at Gowra.

The slaughter on both sides was tremendous. None but old men and boys, it is said, were left in Erin after that fight. The Fianna were in the end almost entirely exterminated, and Oscar slain. He and the King of Ireland, Cairbry, met in single combat, and each of them slew the other. While Oscar was still breathing, though there was not a palm's breadth on his body without a wound, his father found him.

Oscar died, after thanking the gods for his father's safety, and Oisīn and Keelta raised him on a bier of spears and carried him off for burial on the field where he died. Finn took no part in the battle. He is said to have come in a ship to view the field afterwards, and he wept over Oscar, a thing he had never done save once before, for his hound, Bran, whom he himself killed by accident.

CHAPTER VI

THE VOYAGE OF MAELDŪN

Besides the legends which cluster round great heroic names, and have, or at least pretend to have, the character of history, there are many others, great and small, which tell of adventures lying purely in regions of romance, and out of earthly space and time. The "Voyage of Maeldūn" is only one of a number of such wonder-voyages found in ancient Irish literature, but it is believed to have been the earliest of them all and model for the rest.

St Brendan encountering a siren, from *the Marvellous Adventures of St Brendan and his Monks*, 1499, one of the best known of the medieval Irish wonder voyages.

An enormous bird began eating the red berries (opposite). (Illustration by Arthur Rackham, from James Stephens, *Irish Fairy Tales*, 1920.)

THE BIRTH OF MAELDUN

There was a famous man of Aran, named Ailill Edge-of-Battle, who went with his king on a foray into another territory. They encamped one night near a convent of nuns. At midnight Ailill saw a certain nun come out and he caught her by the hand. When they parted, she said to him: "Whence is thy race, and what is thy name?" Said he: "Ailill of the Edge-of-Battle is my name and I am of the Owenacht of Aran." Not long after, he was slain by raiders from Leix.

In due time a son was born to the woman, and she called his name Maeldūn. He was taken secretly to her friend, the queen of the territory, and by her and her husband Maeldūn was reared as if he were their own child till he was a young warrior and fit to use weapons.

One day a proud young warrior who had been defeated by him taunted him with his lack of knowledge of his descent. Maeldūn went to his foster-mother, the queen, and insisted on knowing all, and the queen at last took him to his own mother, the nun, who told him: "Your father was Ailill of the Owens of Aran." Then Maeldūn went to his father's kindred, and was well received by them and with him he took his three foster-brothers, sons of the king and queen who had brought him up.

After a time Maeldūn happened to be among a company of young warriors who were contending at putting the stone in the graveyard of a ruined church. Maeldūn's foot was planted on a scorched and blackened flagstone, and a monk named Briccne, said to him: "It were better to avenge the man who was

Dun Aenghus, stone fort at Inishmore, largest of the Aran Islands from which Maeldun departed on his voyage. Legends say the fort was built by the Fir Bolg.

A coracle of skins. Usually made of hide stretched over a wooden frame, circular boats like these can still be seen on the rivers of Wales and Ireland.

Kenmare Bay, from Templenoe. The seas off this part of south-west Ireland are full of interesting islands, including Skellig Michael, site of an early monastic community. (Illustration by Stephen Gwynn.)

burnt there than to cast stones over his burnt bones."

"Who was that?" asked Maeldún.

"Ailill, your father," they told him.

"Who slew him?" said he.

"Raiders from Leix," they said, "and they destroyed him on this spot."

Then Maeldún went home and he asked the way to Leix. They told him he could only go there by sea.

At the advice of a Druid, he then built him a coracle of skins lapped three-fold one over the other; and the wizard also told him that seventeen men only must accompany him, and on what day he must begin the boat and on what day he must put out to sea.

So when his company was ready, he put out and hoisted the sail, but had gone only a little way when his three foster-brothers came down to the beach and entreated him to take them. "Get you home," said Maeldún, "for none but the number I have may go with me." But the three youths would not be separated from Maeldún, and they flung themselves into the sea. He turned back, lest they should be drowned, and brought them into his boat.

THE VOYAGE

Having set to sea, Maeldún and his party went to a great number of islands and had many strange adventures on them. Those that follow are just some of the places they visited during their long and mysterious voyage.

Maeldún and his crew had rowed all day and half the night when they came to two small bare islands with two forts in them, and a noise was heard from them of armed men quarrelling. "Stand off from me," cried one of them, "for I am a better man than you. I slew Ailill of the Edge-of-Battle and no kins-man has avenged his death on me. And you have never done the like of that."

Then Maeldún was about to land, and German and Diuran the Rhymer cried that God had guided them to the spot where they would be. But a great wind arose suddenly and blew them off into the boundless ocean, and Maeldūn said to his foster-brothers: "You have caused this to be, casting yourselves on board in spite of the words of the Druid." And they had no answer.

They drifted three days and three nights, not knowing whither to row, when at the dawn of the third day they heard the noise of breakers, and came to an island as soon as the sun was up. Here, before they could land, they met a swarm of ferocious ants, each the size of a foal, that came down the strand and into the sea to get at them, so they made off quickly back to sea.. After this they saw no land for three days more.

The Island of the Giant Horses was a great, flat island, which it fell by lot to Germān and Diuran to explore first. They found a vast green racecourse, on which were the marks of horses' hoofs, each as big as a sail, and the shells of nuts of monstrous size were lying about, and much plunder. So they were afraid, and took ship hastily again, and from the sea they saw a horse-race in progress and heard the shouting of a great multitude. So they rowed away with all their might, thinking they had come upon an assembly of demons.

By the time they had come to the Island of The Apples they had been a long time voyaging, and food had failed them, and they were hungry. This island had precipitous sides from which a wood hung down, and as they passed along the cliffs Maeldūn broke off a twig and held it in his hand. Three days and nights they coasted the cliff and found no entrance to the island, but by that time a cluster of three apples had grown on the end of Maeldūn's rod, and each apple sufficed the whole crew for forty days.

The next island had a fence of stone round it, and within the fence a huge beast that raced round and round the island. And anon it went to the top of the island, and then performed a marvellous feat: it turned its body round and round inside its skin, the skin remaining unmoved, while again it would revolve its skin round and round the body. When it saw the party it rushed at them, but they escaped, pelted with stones as they rowed away. One of the stones pierced through Maeldūn's shield and lodged in the keel of the boat.

With great weariness, hunger and thirst they arrived at an island full of trees loaded with golden apples. Under the trees went red beasts, like fiery swine, that kicked the trees with their legs, when the apples fell and the beasts consumed them. The beasts came out at morning only, when a multitude of birds left the island, and swam out to sea till nones, when they turned and swan inward again till vespers, and ate the apples all night.

Maeldūn and his comrades landed at night, and felt the soil hot under their feet from the fiery swine in their caverns underground. They collected all the apples they could, which were good both against hunger and thirst, and loaded their boat with them and put to sea once more, refreshed.

The apples had failed them, when they came hungry and thirsting to the next island. This was, as it were, a tall white tower of chalk reaching up to the clouds, and on the rampart about it were great houses white as snow. They entered the largest of them, and found a small cat playing on four stone pillars which were in the midst of the house. It looked a little on the Irish warriors, but did not cease from its play. On the walls of the houses there were three rows of objects hanging up: one row of brooches of gold and silver, and one of neck-torques of gold and silver, and one of great swords with gold and silver hilts. Quilts and shining garments lay in the room, and there, also, were a roasted ox and a flitch of bacon and abundance of liquor. "Has this been left

A huge beast which "turned its body round and round inside its skin". (Illustration from Standish O'Grady, *Finn and his Companions*, 1892.)

for us?" said Maeldūn to the cat. It looked at him a moment, and then continued its play. So there they ate and drank and slept, and stored up what remained of the food to take with them when they went. Next day, as they made to leave the house, the youngest of Maeldūn's foster-brothers took a necklace from the wall, and was bearing it out when the cat suddenly leaped through him like a fiery arrow, and he fell, a heap of ashes, on the floor. Thereupon Maeldūn replaced the necklace, and they strewed the ashes of the dead youth on the sea-shore, and put to sea again.

The next island had a brazen palisade dividing it in two, and a flock of black sheep on one side and of white sheep on the other. Between them was a big man who tended the flocks, and sometimes he put a white sheep among the black, when it became black at once, or a black sheep among the white, when it immediately turned white. By way of an experiment, Maeldūn flung a peeled white wand on the side of the black sheep. It at once turned black, whereat they left the place in terror, and without landing.

They came to an island full of black people continually weeping and lamenting. One of the two remaining foster-brothers landed on it, and immediately turned black and fell to weeping like the rest. Two others went to fetch him; the same fate befell them. Four others then went with their heads

The youngest of Maeldun's foster-brothers took a necklace. Necklace of glass beads from the Queen's Barrow, Arras (British Museum).

A woman gave them food and drink, all out of her one pail. Wooden bucket with bronze fittings, found at Aylesford, Kent, first century B.C. This pail may have been used as a cremation urn (British Museum.)

wrapped in cloths, that they should not look on the land or breathe the air of the place, and they seized two of the lost ones and brought them away, but not the foster-brother. The two rescued ones could not explain their conduct except by saying that they had to do as they saw others doing about them.

The island they now reached had on it a fortress with a brazen door, and a bridge of glass leading to it. When they sought to cross the bridge it threw them backward. A woman came out of the fortress with a pail in her hand, and let down her pail into the water beneath, and returned to the fortress. They struck on the brazen portcullis to gain admittance, but the melody given forth by the metal plunged them in slumber till the morrow morn. Thrice over, this happened, the woman each time making an ironical speech about Maeldūn. On the fourth day, however, she came out to them over the bridge.

"My welcome, O Maeldūn," she said, and she welcomed each man of the crew by his own name. Then she took them into the great house and gave them abundance of food and drink, all out of her one pail, each man finding in it what he most desired. When she had departed they asked Maeldūn if they should woo the maiden for him. They did so, and she told them they would have their answer tomorrow. When the morning broke, however, they found themselves once more at sea, with no sign of the island or fortress or lady.

Next they found a wooded island full of birds, and on it a solitary man, whose only clothing was his hair. He told them that he was a man of Ireland who had put to sea with a sod of his native country under his feet. God had turned the sod into an island, adding a foot's breadth to it and one tree for every year. He entertained them for three nights, and then they sailed away.

They next found themselves in a sea, thin like mist, that seemed as if it would not support their boat. In the depths they saw roofed fortresses and a fair land around them. A monstrous beast lodged in a tree there, with droves of cattle about it, and beneath it an armed warrior. In spite of the warrior, the beast ever and anon stretched down a long neck and seized one of the cattle and devoured it. Much dreading lest they should sink through that mist-like

In the depths of the sea they saw a monstrous beast. Sea serpent from Olaus Magnus, *Histor. Septentrion.*

St Brendan encounters a holy man from *The Marvellous Adventures of St Brendan and his Monks*, 1499. Many Celtic Christian monks lived as hermits on isolated islands.

The rampart of a mighty fortress. The fort of Dun Aenghus on Inishmore occupies a spectacular site on the edge of a 300 foot high cliff with a sheer drop to the sea on one side and a field of jagged rocks outside its inland walls.

sea, they sailed over it and away. When they arrived on the Island of the Prophecy, they found the water rising in high cliffs round the island, and, looking down, saw on it a crowd of people, who screamed at them, "It is they, it is they," till they were out of breath. Then came a woman and pelted them from below with large nuts, which they gathered and took with them. As they went they heard the folk: "Where are they now?" "They are gone away." "They are not."

The next wonder to which they came was a great silver column, four-square, rising from the sea. Each of its four sides was as wide as two oar-strokes of the boat. Not a sod of earth was at its foot, but it rose from the boundless ocean and its summit was lost in the sky. From that summit a huge silver net was flung far away into the sea, and through a mesh of that net they sailed. As they did so Diuran hacked away a piece of the net. And then they heard a voice from the summit of yonder pillar, mighty, clear and distinct. But they knew not the tongue it spake, or the words it uttered.

On the Island of the Women they found the rampart of a mighty fortress, enclosing a mansion. They landed to look on it and sat on a hillock near by. Within, they saw seventeen maidens busy at preparing a great bath. In a little while a rider, richly clad, came up swiftly on a racehorse, and got down and went inside. The rider then went into the bath, when they saw that it was a woman. Shortly after that one of the maidens came out and said, "The Queen invites you." They went into the fort and bathed and then sat down to meat, each man with a maiden. And Maeldūn was wedded to the queen, and each of the maidens to one of his men. On the morrow they made ready to depart, but the queen would not have them go, and said: "Stay here, and old age will never fall on you, but you shall remain as you are now for ever and ever."

She then told Maeldūn that she was the mother of the seventeen girls they had seen, and her husband had been king of the island. He was now dead, and she reigned in his place. On the morning of each day she went into the great plain in the interior of the island to judge the folk, and returned at night.

So they remained there for three months of winter, but the men wearied of it, and longed to set forth for their own country. At last one day, when the queen was away, they went on board their bark and put out to sea. Before they had gone far, however, the queen came riding up with a ball of twine in her hand, and she flung it after them. Maeldūn caught it in his hand, and it clung to his hand so that he could not free himself, and the queen, holding the other end, drew them back to land. And they stayed on the island another three months.

Twice again the same thing happened, and at last the people averred that Maeldūn held the ball on purpose, so great was his love for the woman. So the next time, another man caught the ball, but it clung to his hand as before, so Diuran smote off his hand, and it fell with the ball into the sea. When she saw that she at once began to wail and shriek, so that all the land was one cry, wailing and shrieking. And thus they escaped from the Island of the Women.

The Island of the Eagle was large, with woods of oak and yew on one side of it, and on the other a plain; there also they found a small church and a fort, and an ancient grey cleric, clad only in his hair. Maeldūn asked him who he was.

An ancient grey cleric claimed to be one of the monks of St Brennan. (Ilustration from "The Voyages of Maeldun", James Stephens, *Irish Fairy Tales*, 1920.)

"I am the fifteenth man of the monks of St. Brennan of Birr," he said. "We went on our pilgrimage into the ocean, and they have all died, save me alone." They stayed there for a season, feeding on the sheep of the island.

One day they saw what seemed to be be a cloud coming up from the south-west. As it drew near, however, they perceived that it was an enormous bird. It came into the island, and, alighting very wearily on a hill near the lake, it began eating the red berries which grew on a huge tree-branch that it had brought with it. And they saw that it was very old, and its plumage dull and decayed.

At the hour of noon, two eagles came up from the south-west and alit in front of the great bird, and set to work picking off the insects that infested its jaws and eyes and ears. At last, on the following day, when the great bird had been completely cleansed, it plunged into the lake, and again the two eagles picked and cleansed it. On the third day its feathers became glossy and abundant, and then, soaring upwards, it flew thrice round the island, and away to the quarter whence it had come, and its flight was now swift and strong.

Then Diuran said: "Let us bathe in that lake and renew ourselves where the bird hath been renewed." He plunged in and drank of the water. From that time so long as he lived his eyes were strong and keen, and not a tooth fell from his jaw nor a hair from his head, and he never knew illness or infirmity.

On the Island of the Laughing Folk they found a great company of men laughing and playing incessantly. They drew lots as to who should enter and explore it, and it fell to Maeldūn's foster-brother. But when he set foot on it he at once began to laugh and play with the others, and could not leave off, nor would he come back to his comrades. So they left him and sailed away.

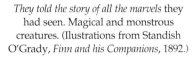

They told the story of all the marvels they had seen. Magical and monstrous creatures. (Illustrations from Standish O'Grady, Finn and his Companions, 1892.)

The Island of the Falcon was uninhabitated, save for herds of sheep and oxen. They landed on it and ate their fill, and one of them saw there a large falcon. "This falcon", he said, "is like the falcons of Ireland." "Watch it," said Maeldūn, "and see how it will go from us." It flew off to the south-east, and they rowed after it all day till vespers.

THE HOME-COMING

At nightfall they sighted a land like Ireland, and soon came to a small island, where they went ashore. It was there dwelt the man who had slain Ailill.

They went up to the fortress that was on the island, and heard men talking within it as they sat at meat. One man said:

"It would be ill for us if we saw Maeldūn now."

"That Maeldūn has been drowned," said another.

"If he should come now", said another, "what should we do?"

"Not hard to answer that," said the chief of them. "Great welcome should he have if he were to come, for he hath been a long space in great tribulation."

Then Maeldūn smote with the wooden clapper against the door. "Who is there?" asked the doorkeeper.

"Maeldūn is here," said he.

They entered the house in peace, and great welcome was made for them, and they were arrayed in new garments. And then they told the story of all the marvels they had seen.

la ueille de la pentecou
ste qnt tout li compaig

CHAPTER VII

MYTHS AND TALES OF THE CYMRY

T he myths and legends of the Celtic race which have come down to us in the Welsh language are in some respects of a different character from those which we possess in Gaelic. The Welsh material is nothing like as full as the Gaelic, nor so early. The tales of the *Mabinogion* are mainly drawn from the fourteenth-century manuscript entitled "The Red Book of Hergest." (*Mabinogion* is the plural form of the word *Mabinogi*, which means a story belonging to the repertoire of an apprentice bard.) One of them, the romance of Taliesin, came from another source, a manuscript of the seventeenth century. The four oldest tales in the *Mabinogion* are supposed by scholars to have taken their present shape in the tenth or eleventh century, while several Irish tales, like the story of Etain and Midir or the Death of Conary, go back to the seventh or eighth. As one might therefore expect, the mythological elements in the Welsh romances are usually much more confused and harder to decipher than in the earlier of the Irish tales. The mythic interest has grown less, the story interest greater; the object of the bard is less to hand down a sacred text than to entertain a prince's court. We must remember also that the influence of the Continental romances of chivalry is clearly perceptible in the Welsh tales, and in fact, comes eventually to govern them completely.

GODS OF THE HOUSE OF DŌN

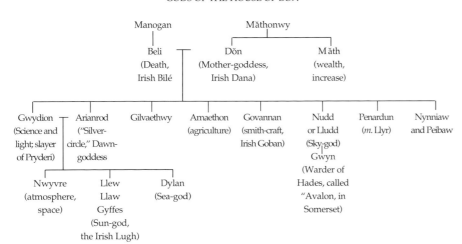

Arthur and his court at a feast (opposite), as imagined by a medieval illustrator. A figure in the foreground appears to be reading to the company. (British Library.)

101

GODS OF THE HOUSE OF LLYR

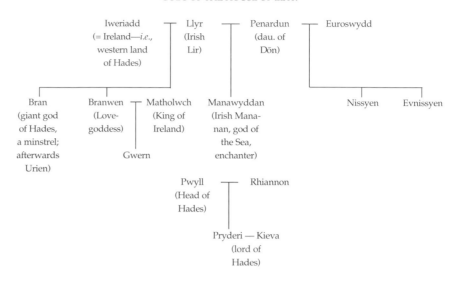

ARTHUR AND HIS KIN

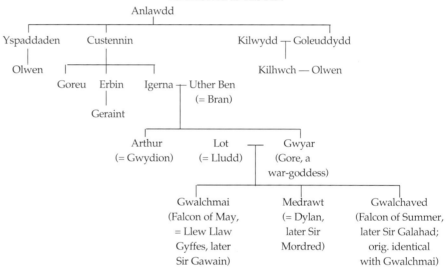

Don, a mother-goddess. This female figure with birds and children from the Gundestrup cauldron is widely assumed to represent a Celtic goddess of fertility and plenty. (National Museum of Denmark.)

Llanfair-ar-y-Bryn, a typical Dyfed landscape. In the days of Pwyll, Dyfed consisted of seven cantrevs, or seven times one hundred homesteads.

Two great divine houses or families are discernible: that of Dōn, a mother-goddess (representing the Gaelic Dana), whose husband is Beli, the Irish Bilé, god of Death, and whose descendants are the Children of Light; and the House of Llyr, the Gaelic Lir, who here represents, not a Danaan deity, but something more like the Irish Fomorians. As in the case of the Irish myth, the two families are allied by intermarriage—Penardun, a daughter of Dōn, is wedded to Lyr. Dōn herself has a brother, Māth, whose name signifies wealth or treasure, and they descend from a figure indistinctly characterized, called Māthonwy.

The genealogical tables show these connections and the relations between Welsh and Irish counterparts more clearly.

THE HOUSE OF LLYR

The first of the *Mabinogion* tells the story of Pwyll, Prince of Dyfed, and how that prince got his title of *Pen Annwn*, or "Head of Hades."

Pwyll, it is said, was hunting one day in the woods of Glyn Cuch when he saw a pack of hounds, not his own, running down a stag. He drove off the strange hounds, and was setting his own on the quarry when a horseman of noble appearance came up and reproached him for his discourtesy, so Pwyll offered to make amends. The stranger's name was Arawn, a king in Annwn. He was being harried and dispossessed by a rival, Havgan, and he sought the aid of Pwyll, whom he begged to meet Havgan in single combat a year hence. Meanwhile he would put his own shape on Pwyll, who was to rule in his king-

dom till the eventful day, while Arawn was to go in Pwyll's shape to govern Dyfed. He instructed Pwyll how to deal with the foe. Havgan had to be laid low with a single stroke, which he would not survive. If another was given to him he immediately revived again as strong as ever.

Pwyll accordingly went in Arawn 's shape to the kingdom of Annwn. The beautiful wife of Arawn greeted him as her husband. But when the time came for them to retire to rest he set his face to the wall and said no word to her, nor touched her at all until the morning broke. Then they rose up, and Pwyll went to the hunt, and ruled his kingdom, and did all things as if he were monarch of the land, but he passed every night even as this first.

At last the day of battle came, and Pwyll and Havgan met each other in the midst of a river-ford. They fought and at the first clash Havgan fell mortally wounded. "For the love of heaven", said he, "slay me and complete your work." "I may yet repent that," said Pwyll. "Slay you who may, I will not." Then Havgan knew that his end was come, and bade his nobles bear him off, and Pwyll with all his army overran the two kingdoms of Annwn, and made himself master of all the land.

Then he rode off alone to keep his tryst in Glyn Cuch with Arawn as they had appointed. Arawn thanked him for all he had done, and added: "When

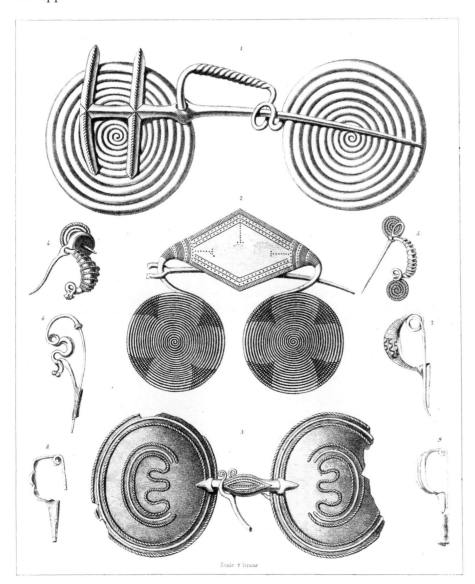

Celtic bronze fibulae (left) were used to pin together such garments as cloaks and capes. (Illustration from Kemble, Franks and Latham, *Horae Ferales*, 1863.)

The kingdom of Annwn (opposite) is a magical otherworld, like the Avalon to which King Arthur is taken after death. (Detail of a painting by Sir Edward Burne-Jones, Museo de Arte, Ponce, Puetro Rico.)

you come to your own dominions you will see what I have done for you." They exchanged shapes once more, and each rode to his own land.

At the court of Annwn the day was spent in joy and feasting, though none but Arawn himself knew that anything unusual had taken place. When night came, Arawn kissed and caressed his wife as of old, and she pondered much as to what might be the cause of his change towards her. "I tell you," she said, "for a year back there has been neither converse nor tenderness between us." Then Arawn told his queen what had passed. "You have indeed laid hold of a faithful friend," she said.

And Pwyll when he came back to his own land called his lords together and asked them how they thought he had sped in his kingship during the past year. "Lord," said they, "your wisdom was never so great, and you were never so kind and free in bestowing your gifts, and your justice was never more worthily seen than in this year."

So the two kings made strong the friendship that was between them, and in memory of the adventure Pwyll bore thenceforward the title of "Lord of Annwn" and the name "Lord of Dyfed" fell into disuse.

Epona, the Celtic horse goddess, is generally identified with Rhiannon, the Welsh princess first seen riding a white horse and later condemned to do the work of a mare.

Rhiannon

Near to the castle of Narberth, where Pwyll had his court, there was a mound called the Mound of Arberth, of which it was believed that whoever sat upon it would either receive blows and wounds or he would see a wonder. One day when all his lords were assembled at Narberth for a feast Pwyll declared that he would sit on the mound and see what would befall.

He did so, and after a little while saw approaching him along the road that led to the mound a lady clad in garments that shone like gold, and sitting on a pure white horse. "Is there any among you", said Pwyll to his men, "who knows that lady?" "There is not," said they. "Then go to meet her and learn who she is." But as they rode towards the lady she moved away from them, and however fast they rode she still kept an even distance between her and them all the time going at the same pace.

Next day Pwyll ascended the mound again, and once more the fair lady on her white steed drew near. This time Pwyll himself pursued her, but she flitted away before him till at last he cried: "O maiden, for the sake of him you best love stay for me." "I will stay gladly," said she.

Pwyll then questioned her as to the cause of her coming, and she said: "I am Rhiannon, the daughter of Hevydd Hēn, and they sought to give me to a husband against my will. But no husband would I have, and that because of my love for you, neither will I yet have one if you reject me." "By heaven!" said Pwyll, "if I might choose among all the ladies and damsels of the world, you would I choose."

They then agreed that in a twelvemonth from that day Pwyll was to come and claim her at the palace of Hevydd Hēn.

Pwyll kept his tryst, with a following of a hundred knights, and found a splendid feast prepared for him. As they feasted, there entered a tall, auburn-haired youth of royal bearing, who saluted Pwyll and his knights. "I am a suitor," said the youth, "to crave a boon am I come." "Whatever have," said Pwyll unsuspiciously, "if it be in my power." "Ah," cried Rhiannon, "why did you give that answer?" "Has he not given it before all these nobles?" said the youth, "and now the boon I crave is to have your bride Rhiannon, and the feast and the banquet that are in this place." Pwyll was silent. "Be silent as long as you will," said Rhiannon. "Never did man make worse use of his wits than you have done." She told him that the auburn-haired young man was Gwawl, son of Clud, and was the suitor to escape from whom she had fled to Pwyll.

Pwyll was bound in honour by his word, and Rhiannon said that in a twelvemonth Gwawl was to come and claim her, and a new bridal feast would be prepared for him. Meantime she made a plan with Pwyll, and gave him a certain magical bag, which he was to make use of when the time came.

A year passed away, Gwawl appeared and a great feast was again set forth, in which he, and not Pwyll, had the place of honour. As the company were making merry, however, a beggar came into the hall, carrying a bag. He humbly craved a boon of Gwawl that the fill of his bag of food might be given him from the banquet. Gwawl cheerfully consented, but however much they put into it, it never got fuller, and at last Gwawl cried: "My soul, will your bag never be full?" "It will not, I declare to heaven," answered Pwyll—for he, of course, was the disguised beggar man—"unless some wealthy man shall get into the bag and stamp it down with his feet, and declare, 'Enough has been put herein.' " Gwawl put his two feet into it; Pwyll immediately drew up the sides of the bag over Gwawl's head and tied it up.

Gwawl put his two feet into the bag, whereupon Pwyll, disguised as a beggar, tied him inside it. (Illustration by Joan Kiddell-Monroe.)

Rhiannon carries strangers into the castle on her back as punishment for a crime that she did not commit. (Detail of illustration by Dorothea Braby.)

Then he blew his horn, and the knights he had with him, who were concealed outside, rushed in, and captured and bound the followers of Gwawl. "What is in the bag?" they cried, and others answered, "A badger", and so they played the game of "Badger in the Bag," striking it and kicking it about the hall.

At last a voice was heard from it. "Lord," cried Gwawl, "if you would but hear me, I merit not to be slain in a bag." "He speaks truth," said Hevydd Hēn.

So an agreement was come to that Gwawl should abandon Rhiannon, and never seek to have revenge for what had been done to him. Gwawl and his men were released and went to their own territory. And Pwyll wedded Rhiannon, and they journeyed down to the palace of Narberth in Dyfed, where they ruled the land in peace.

A son was born to Pwyll and Rhiannon. But although six women sat up to watch the mother and the infant, towards morning they all fell asleep, and when the women awoke, the boy was gone! "We shall be burnt for this," said the women, and in their terror they killed a cub of a staghound and laid the bones by Rhiannon, and smeared her face and hands with blood as she slept, and they said she had devoured her child in the night.

When the story was told to Pwyll, he would not put away Rhiannon but a penance was imposed on her—namely, that she was to sit every day by the horse-block at the gate of the castle and tell the tale to every stranger who came, and offer to carry them on her back into the castle. And this she did for part of a year.

Now at this time there lived a man named Teirnyon of Gwent Is Coed, who had the most beautiful mare in the world, but although she foaled on the night of every first of May, none ever knew what became of the colts. The next night on which the mare should foal he armed himself and watched in the stable. So the mare foaled, and the colt stood up, and Teirnynon was admiring it when a great noise was heard outside, and a long, clawed arm came through the window of the stable and laid hold of the colt. Teirnyon immediately smote at the arm with his sword, and severed it at the elbow, so that it fell inside with the colt, and a great wailing was heard outside. He rushed out, leaving the door open behind him, but could see nothing. Then he came back, and behold, at the door he found an infant wrapped in a mantle of satin. He took up the child and brought it to where his wife lay sleeping. She had no children, and next day pretended to her women that she had borne it as her own. And they called its name Gwri of the Golden Hair, for its hair was yellow as gold.

While these things were going on, Teirnyon heard the tale of Rhiannon and her punishment. And as the lad grew up he saw that he had the features of Pwyll, Prince of Dyfed. This he told to his wife, and they agreed that the child should be taken to Narberth, and Rhiannon released from her penance.

As they drew near to the castle, Teirnyon and two knights and the child, there was Rhiannon, sitting by the horse-block. "Chieftains", said she, "go no further thus; I will bear every one of you into the palace, and this is my penance for slaying my own son and devouring him." But they would not be carried, and went in. Pwyll rejoiced to see Teirnyon, and made a feast for him. Afterwards, Teirnyon declared to Pwyll and Rhiannon the adventure of the man and the colt, and how they had found the boy. "And behold, here is your son, lady," said Teirnyon, "and whoever told that lie concerning you has done wrong." All who sat at table recognized the lad at once as the child of Pwyll, and a chief named Pendaran said: "Well have you named your son Pryderi [trouble], and well becomes him the name of Pryderi, son of Pwyll, Lord of Annwn." It was agreed that his name should be Pryderi, and he was trained

Teirnyon found the infant Gwri wrapped in a mantle of satin and took him to Pwyll. (Illustration by John D. Batten from Joseph Jacobs, *Celtic Fairy Tales*, 1894.)

Bronze harness fitting, decorated with red enamel, from Polden Hill, Somerset. Such mounts could be attached to a strap and used to decorate a chariot horse. (British Museum.)

up, as befitted a king's son, and when his father Pwyll died he reigned in his stead over the Seven Cantrevs of Dyfed. And he added to them many other fair dominions, and at last he took to wife Kicva, daughter of Gwynn Gohoyw, who came of the lineage of Prince Casnar of Britain.

The Tale of Bran and Branwen

Bendigeid Vran, or "Bran the Blessed", when he had been made King of the Isle of the Mighty (Britain), was one time in his court at Harlech. And he had with him his brother Manawyddan, son of Llyr, and his sister Branwen, and the two sons, Nissyen and Evnissyen, that Penardun his mother bore to Eurosswyd. Now Nissyen was a youth of gentle nature, but Evnissyen loved nothing so much as to turn peace into contention and strife.

One afternoon, as Bran sat on the rock of Harlech looking out to sea, he beheld thirteen ships coming rapidly from Ireland before a fair wind, and on the foremost ship, when they came near, a man could be seen holding up a shield with the point upwards, in sign of peace.

When the strangers landed, they saluted Bran and explained their business. Matholwch, King of Ireland, was with them; he had come to ask for the hand in marriage of Bran's sister, Branwen, so that Ireland and Britain might be leagued together and both become more powerful.

The Irish were hospitably entertained, and after taking counsel with his lords, Bran agreed to give his sister to Matholwch. The place of the wedding was fixed at Aberffraw, and the company assembled for the feast in tents because no house could hold the giant form of Bran. They caroused and made merry in peace and amity, and Branwen became the bride of the Irish king.

Next day Evnissyen came by chance to where the horses of Matholwch were ranged, and he asked whose they were. "They are the horses of Mathol-wch, who is married to your sister." "And is it thus", said he, "they have done with a maiden such as she, and, moreover, my sister, bestowing her without my consent? They could offer me no greater insult." Thereupon he rushed among the horses and cut off their lips at the teeth, and their ears to their

Bran sat on the rock of Harlech. The shallow beaches on this west-facing stretch of the Welsh coast provided safe landing places for ships from Ireland.

Castel Dinas Bran, a fortress on a high crag overlooking the Vale of Llangollen, is named after the Welsh hero Bran. No traces of his castle at Aberffraw have yet been found.

heads, and their tails close to the body, and where he could seize the eyelids he cut them off to the bone so that they were of no use to anyone.

When Matholwch heard what had been done he was both angered and bewildered, and bade his people put to sea. Bran sent Manawyddan and two others to make atonement. Matholwch should have sound horses for every one that was injured, and in addition, a staff of silver as large and as tall as himself, and a plate of gold the size of his face. But as for Evnissyen, he was the son of Bran's mother, and therefore Bran could not put him to death as he deserved.

Matholwch accepted these terms, but not very cheerfully, and Bran now offered another treasure; namely, a magic cauldron which had the property that if a slain man were cast into it he would come forth well and sound, only he would not be able to speak. Matholwch and Bran then talked about the cauldron, which originally came from Ireland.

So Matholwch received the cauldron along with his bride, and sailed back to Ireland, where Branwen entertained the lords and ladies of the land. And when the year was out Branwen bore a son to Matholwch, whose name was called Gwern and who was sent to be fostered.

In the second year, it appears, and not till then, the men of Ireland grew indignant over the insult to their king committed by Evnissyen, and took revenge for it by having Branwen degraded to the position of a cook. They also forbade all ships and ferry-boats to cross to Cambria, and any who came thence into Ireland were imprisoned so that news of Branwen's ill-treatment might not come to the ears of Bran. But Branwen reared up a young starling in a corner of her kneading-trough, and one day she tied a letter under its wing

The gilt silver cauldron from Gundestrup in Denmark. Consisting of embossed plates welded together, it measures about 70 cm across the rim. (National Museum of Denmark.)

Envissyen laid his hand on the bag and squeezed it until he had killed the man inside. (Illustration from T. W. H. Rolleston, *Myths of the Celtic Race*, 1911.)

and taught it what to do. It flew away towards Britain, and finding Bran at Caer Seiont in Arvon, it lit on his shoulder, and the letter was found and read. Bran immediately prepared a great host for Ireland, and sailed thither with a fleet of ships, leaving Britain under his son Caradawc and six other chiefs.

Soon there came messengers to Matholwch, telling him of a wondrous sight they had seen; a wood was growing on the sea, and beside the wood a mountain with a high ridge in the middle of it. And wood and mountain moved towards the shore of Ireland. Branwen was called up to explain, if she could, what this meant. She told them the wood was the masts and yards of the fleet of Britain, and the mountain was Bran, her brother.

The King of Ireland and his lords at once took counsel together, and the plan they agreed upon was as follows: A huge hall should be built, big enough to hold Bran, there should be a great feast made there for himself and his men, and Matholwch should give over the kingdom of Ireland to him and do homage. All this was done by Branwen's advice. But the Irish added a crafty device of their own. From two brackets on each of the hundred pillars in the hall should be hung two leather bags, with an armed warrior in each of them ready to fall upon the guests when the moment should arrive.

Evnissyen, however, wandered into the hall before the rest of the host, and scanning the arrangements he saw the bags. "What is in this bag?" said he to one of the Irish. "Meal, good soul", said the Irishman. Evnissyen laid his hand on the bag, and felt about with his fingers till he came to the head of the man within it. Then he squeezed the head till he felt his fingers meet together in the brain through the bone, and thus he did with all the two hundred bags.

Then the feasting began, and concord reigned, and Matholwch laid down the sovereignty of Ireland, which was conferred on the boy Gwern. And they all caressed the fair child till he came to Evnissyen, who suddenly seized him and flung him into the blazing fire on the hearth. Branwen would have leaped after him, but Bran held her back. Then there was arming apace, and tumult and shouting, and the Irish and British hosts closed in battle and fought until the fall of night.

But at night the Irish heated the magic cauldron and threw into it the bodies of their dead, who came out next day as good as ever, but dumb. When Evnissyen saw this he was smitten with remorse for having brought the men of Britain into such a strait. So he hid himself among the Irish dead, and was flung into the cauldron with the rest, at the end of the second day, when he stretched himself out so that he rent the cauldron into four pieces, and his own heart burst with the effort, and he died.

In the end, all the Irishmen were slain, and all but seven of the British besides Bran, who was wounded in the foot with a poisoned arrow. Among the seven were Pryderi and Manawyddan. Bran then commanded them to cut off his head. "And take it with you," he said, "to London, and there bury it in the White Mount looking towards France, and no foreigner shall invade the land while it is there. On the way, the Head will talk to you and be as pleasant company as ever in life. In Harlech you will be feasting seven years and the birds of Rhiannon will sing to you. And at Gwales in Penvro, you will be feasting fourscore years, and the Head will talk to you and be uncorrupted till you

After looking towards Cornwall the British had to leave Penvro, or Pembroke, for London. Standing stones near Minions in Cornwall are said to be men changed into stone for playing at hurling on a Sunday.

Harlech Castle as it now stands was built in the thirteenth century, but beneath the present castle is evidence of an earlier Celtic fortress.

Heads on a silver disc from Manerbia sul Mella, Italy. Thought to be a horse decoration, the disc was probably used as a charm to ward off evil through the magical powers of the heads.

open the door looking towards Cornwall. After that you may no longer tarry, but set forth immediately to London and bury the Head." Then the seven cut off the head of Bran and went forth, and Branwen with them, to do his bidding. But when Branwen came to land at Aber Alaw she cried, "Woe is me that I was ever born; two islands have been destroyed because of me." And she uttered a loud groan, and her heart broke. The seven found that in the absence of Bran, Caswallan, son of Beli, had conquered Britain and slain the six captains of Caradawc. By magic art, he had thrown on Caradawc the Veil of Illusion, and Caradawc saw only the sword which slew and slew, but not him who wielded it, and his heart broke for grief at the sight.

They then went to Harlech and remained there seven years listening to the singing of the birds of Rhiannon. Then they went to Gwales in Penvro and found a fair and spacious hall overlooking the ocean. When they entered it they forgot all the sorrow of the past and remained there fourscore years in joy and mirth, the wondrous Head talking to them as if it were alive. Three doors were in the hall, and one of them which looked to Cornwall and to Aber Henvelyn was closed, but the other two were open. At the end of the time, Heilyn, son of Gwyn, said, "Evil betide me if I do not open the door to see if what was said is true." And he opened it, and at once remembrance and sorrow fell upon them, and they set forth at once for London and buried the Head in the White Mount, where it remained until Arthur dug it up, for he would not have the land defended but by the strong arm.

The Tale of Pryderi and Manawyddan

After the events of the previous tales, Pryderi and Manawyddan retired to the dominions of the former, and Manawyddan took to wife Rhiannon, the mother of his friend. There they lived happily and prosperously till one day, while they were at the Gorsedd, near Narberth, a peal of thunder was heard and a thick mist fell so that nothing could be seen all round. When the mist cleared away, all was desert and uninhabited. The palace of Narberth was still standing, but it was empty and desolate—none remained except Pryderi and Manawydan and their wives, Kicva and Rhiannon.

Two years they lived on the provisions they had, and on the prey they killed, and on wild honey, and then they began to be weary. "Let us go into Lloegyr," then said Manawyddan, "and seek out some craft to support ourselves." So they went to Hereford and settled there, and Manawyddan and Pryderi began to make saddles and housings. After a time, however, the other saddlers of Hereford, finding that no man would purchase any but the work of Manawyddan, conspired to kill them. And Pryderi would have fought with them, but Manawyddan held it better to withdraw elsewhere.

They settled then in another city, where they made shields and here, too, the rival craftsmen drove them out. And this happened also in another town where they made shoes, and at last they resolved to go back to Dyfed. Then they gathered their dogs about them and lived by hunting as before.

One day they started a wild white boar, and chased him to a vast and lofty

Pryderi found a marble fountain, but when he put his hand on the bowl beside it he became stuck fast. (Illustration by John. D. Batten to Joseph Jacobs, *Celtic Fairy Tales*, 1894.)

Bronze shields. The bronze piece was usually no more than a decorative cover for a wooden framework, rather than being a defence in itself. (Illustration from Kemble, Franks and Latham, *Horae Ferales*, 1863.)

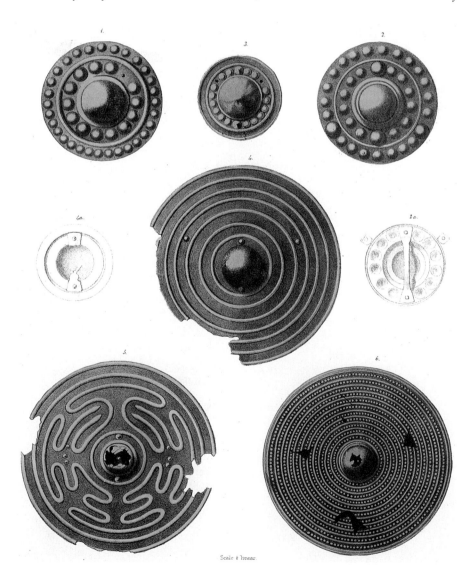

115

A mighty host of mice ate the wheat crop that Manawydan had sown. (Illustration by John. D. Batten to Joseph Jacobs, *Celtic Fairy Tales*, 1892.)

Gold stater of Cunobelin, a Celtic leader during the Roman occupation of Britain, who issued his own coins from Camulodunum (now Colchester) and Verulamium (now St. Alban's).

The reverse of the coin shows an ear of corn. Cunobelin is assumed to be the model for Shakespeare's Cymbeline.

castle. Pryderi, against the counsel of Manawyddan, who knew there was magic afoot, went in to seek for the dogs. He found in the centre of the court a marble fountain beside which stood a golden bowl on a marble slab, and laid hold of it to examine it, when he could neither withdraw his hand nor utter a single sound, but he remained there, transfixed and dumb, beside the fountain.

Manawyddan went back to Narberth and told the story to Rhiannon. "An evil companion have you been," said she, "and a good companion have you lost." Next day, she went herself to explore the castle. She found Pryderi still clinging to the bowl and unable to speak. She also, then, laid hold of the bowl, when the same fate befell her, and immediately afterwards came a peal of thunder, and a heavy mist fell, and when it cleared off the castle had vanished with all that it contained, including the two spell-bound wanderers.

Manawyddan then went back to Narberth, where only Kicva, Pryderi's wife, now remained. Kicva and Manawyddan again tried to support themselves by shoemaking in Lloegyr, but the same hostility drove them back to Dyfed. This time, however, Manawydan took back with him a load of wheat, and he sowed it, and he prepared three crofts for a wheat crop. Thus the time passed till the fields were ripe, and he looked at one of the crofts and said, "I will reap this to-morrow." But on the morrow when he went out in the grey dawn he found nothing there but bare straw—every ear had been cut off from the stalk and carried away.

Next day it was the same with the second croft. But on the following night he armed himself and sat up to watch the third croft to see who was plundering him. At midnight, he heard a loud noise; a mighty host of mice came pouring into the croft, climbed up each on a stalk and nibbled off the ears and made away with them. He chased them in anger, but they fled far faster than he could run, all save one which was slower in its movements, and this he bound into his glove and took it home to Narberth, and told Kicva what had hapened. "To-morrow", he said, "I will hang the robber I have caught," but Kicva thought it beneath his dignity to take vengeance on a mouse.

Next day he went up to the Mound of Narberth and set up two forks for a gallows on the highest part of the hill. As he was doing this a poor scholar came towards him and begged him to let go the mouse. "I will not let it go, by Heaven," said Manawyddan, although the scholar offered him a pound of money to let it go free. As Manawyddan was placing the cross-beam on the gallows, a priest came towards him riding on a horse with trappings, and the same conversation ensued. The priest offered three pounds for the mouse's life, but Manawyddan refused to take any price for it.

Then Manawyddan put a noose about the mouse's neck and was about to draw it up when he saw coming towards him a bishop with a great retinue of sumpter-horses and attendants. The bishop offered seven pounds "rather than see a man of thy rank destroying so vile a reptile." Manawyddan refused. Four-and-twenty pounds was then offered, and then as much again, then all the bishop's horses and baggage—all in vain. "Since for this you will not," said the bishop, "do it at whatever price you will." "I will do so," said Manawyddan; "I will that Rhiannon and Pryderi be free." "That you shall have," said the (pretended) bishop. Then Manawyddan demanded that the enchantment and illusion be taken off for ever from the seven Cantrevs of Dyfed, and finally insisted that the bishop tell him who the mouse was and why the enchantment was laid on the country. "I am Llwyd, son of Kilcoed," replied the enchanter, "and the mouse is my wife; but that she is pregnant you had never overtaken her." The charm was cast on the land to avenge the ill that was done Llwyd's friend, Gwawl, son of Clud, with whom Pryderi's father and his knights had played "Badger in the Bag" at the court of Hevydd Hēn. The mice were the lords and ladies of Llwyd's court.

The enchanter was then made to promise that no further vengeance should be taken on Pryderi, Rhiannon or Manawyddan, and the two spell-bound captives having been restored, the mouse was released. Then Llwyd struck her with a magic wand, and she was changed into a young woman, the fairest ever seen.

THE HOUSE OF DŌN

Māth, the lord of Gwynedd, was unable to exist unless his feet lay in the lap of a maiden, except when the land was disturbed by war. His nephews Gwydion and Gilvaethwy, sons of Dōn, went the circuit of the land in his stead, while Māth lay with his feet in the lap of the fairest maiden of the land and time, Goewin, daughter of Pebin of Dōl Pebin in Arvon.

Gilvaethwy fell sick of love for Goewin, and confided the secret to his brother Gwydion, who undertook to help him to his desire. So he went to Māth one day, and asked his leave to go to Pryderi and beg from him the gift, for Māth, of a herd of swine which had been bestowed on him by Arawn, King of Annwn. Māth bade him go, and he and Gilvaethwy started with ten companions for Dyfed. They came to Pryderi's palace in the guide of bards, and Gwydion was asked to tell a tale to the court. After delighting every one with his discourse, he begged for a gift of the swine. But Pryderi was under a compact with his people neither to sell nor give them until they had produced double their number in the land. "You may exchange them, though," said Gwydion, and thereupon he made by magic arts an illusion of twelve horses and twelve hounds, and gave them to Pryderi and made off with the swine as fast as possible, "for", said he to his companions, "the illusion will not last but from one hour to the same to-morrow."

Pryderi invaded the land to recover his swine, Māth went to meet him in arms, and Gilvaethwy seized his opportunity and made Goewin his wife, although she was unwilling.

The war was decided by a single combat between Gwydion and Pryderi. And by force of strength and fierceness, and by the magic and charms of Gwydion, Pryderi was slain. And at Maen Tyriawc, above Melenryd, was he buried.

When Māth came back he found what Gilvaethwy had done, and he took Goewin to be his queen, but Gwydion and Gilvaethwy went into outlawry, and dwelt on the borders of the land. At last they came and submitted themselves for punishment to Māth. So he turned them both into deer, and bade them come hither again in a twelvemonth.

They came at the appointed time, bringing with them a young fawn. And the fawn was brought into human shape and baptized, and Gwydion and Gilvaethwy were changed into two wild swine. At the next years's end, they came back with a young one who was treated as the fawn before him, and the brothers were made into wolves. Another year passed; they came back again

Disguised as bards, Gwydion and Gilvaethwy went to Pryderi's palace. (Illustration from C. Hamilton Smith, *Ancient Customes of Great Britain and Ireland*, 1814.)

Single combat between Gwydion and Pryderi ended in the death of Pryderi. (Illustration by Stephen Reid from T. W. H. Rolleston, *Myths of the Celtic Race*, 1911.)

Dylan, a sea-deity. Sitting astride a dolpin, a figure from the Gundestrup cauldron demonstrates his connections with the sea. (National Museum of Denmark.)

Green Bridge of Wales, Castlemartin, Dyfed. Legends of a secret passage have grown up around this natural stone arch on the south-west coast of Wales.

with a young wolf as before, and this time their human nature was restored to them, and Māth gave orders to have them washed and anointed and nobly clad as was befitting.

The question then arose of appointing another virgin foot-holder, and Gwydion suggested his sister, Arianrod. She attended for the purpose, and Māth asked her if she were a virgin. "I know not, lord, other than that I am," she says. But she failed in a magical test imposed by Māth, and gave birth to two sons. One of these was named Dylan, "Son of the Wave", a sea-deity. So soon as he was baptized "he plunged into the sea and swam as well as the best fish that was therein. … Beneath him no wave ever broke." On his death, which took place, it is said, at the hand of his uncle Govannon, all the waves of Britain and Ireland wept for him.

Llew Llaw Gyffes

Arianrod's other child was seized by Gwydion and brought up under his protection. One day Gwydion took him to visit his mother. "What is his name?" she asked. "Verily", said Gwydion, "he has not yet a name." "Then I lay this destiny upon him," said Arianrod, "that he shall never have a name till one is given him by me."

Gwydion, who was the father of Arianrod's children was resolved to have a name for his son. Next day he went to the strand below Caer Arianrod, bringing the boy with him. Here he sat down by the beach, and in his character of a master of magic he made himself look like a shoemaker, and the boy like an apprentice, and he began to make shoes out of sedges and seaweed, to which he gave the semblance of leather. Word was brought to Arianrod of the wonderful shoes and she came to be fitted. While this was going on, a wren came and lit on the boat's mast, and the boy, taking up a bow, shot an arrow that transfixed the leg between the sinew and the bone. Arianrod admired the brilliant shot. "Verily," she said, "with a steady hand (*llaw gyffes*) did the lion (*llew*) hit it." "No thanks to you," cried Gwydion, "now you have given the boy a name. Llew Llaw Gyffes shall he be called henceforward."

The shoes turned immediately to sedges and seaweed again, and Arianrod, angry at being tricked, laid a new curse on the boy. "He shall never bear arms till I invest him with them." But Gwydion, going to Caer Arianrod with the boy in the semblance of two bards, made by magic art the illusion of a foray of armed men round the castle. Arianrod gave them weapons to help in the defence, and thus again found herself tricked by the superior craft of Gwydion.

Next she said, "He shall never have a wife of the race that now inhabits this earth." This raised a difficulty beyond the powers of even Gwydion, and he went to Māth, the supreme master of magic. "Well", said Māth, "we will seek, I and you, to form a wife for him out of flowers." So they took the blossoms of the oak, and the blossoms of the broom, and the blossoms of the meadow-sweet, and produced from them a maiden, the fairest and most graceful that man ever saw. And they gave her the name of Blodeuwedd, or Flower-face. They wedded her to Llew, and gave them the cantrev of Dinodig to reign over, and there Llew and his bride dwelt for a season, happy, and beloved by all.

But Blodeuwedd was not worthy of her beautiful name and origin. One day when Llew was away on a visit with Māth, a lord named Gronw Pebyr came hunting by the palace of Llew, and Blodeuwedd loved him from the moment she looked upon him. That night they slept together, and the next, and the next, and then they planned how to be rid of Llew for ever. But Llew was invulnerable except under special circumstances, and Blodeuwedd had to learn from him how he might be slain under pretence of care for his welfare. The problem was a hard one. Llew could only be killed by a spear which had been a year in making, and had only been worked on during the Sacrifice of the Host on Sundays. Furthermore, he could not be slain within a house or without, on horseback or on foot. The only way, in fact, was that he should stand with one foot on a dead buck and the other in a cauldron, which was to be used for a bath and thatched with a roof—if he was wounded while in this position with a spear made as directed, the wound might be fatal, not other-wise. After a year, during which Gronw wrought at the spear, Blodeuwedd begged Llew to show her the required position to please her. Gronw hurled the deadly spear, and the head, which was poisoned, sank into Llew's body but the shaft broke off. Then Llew changed into an eagle, soared up into the air and was no more seen.

These tidings at last reached Gwydion and Māth, and Gwydion set out to find Llew. He came to the house of a vassal of his, from whom he learned that a sow that he had disappeared every day and could not be traced, but it came home duly each night. Gwydion followed the sow, and it went far away to the brook since called Nant y Llew, where it stopped under a tree and began feed-ing. Gwydion looked to see what it ate, and found that it fed on putrid flesh that dropped from an eagle sitting aloft on the tree, and it seemed to him that the eagle was Llew. Gwydion sang to it, and brought it gradually down the tree till it came to his knee, when he struck it with his magic wand and restored it to the shape of Llew, but worn to skin and bone.

When Llew was healed, he and Gwydion took vengeance on their foes. Blodeuwedd was changed into an owl and bidden to shun the light of day, and Gronw was slain by a cast of the spear of Llew that passed through a slab of stone to reach him. And Llew took possession for the second time of his lands, and ruled them prosperously all his days.

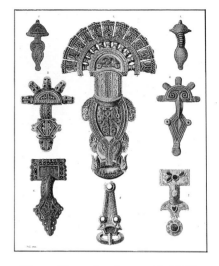

Silver and bronze brooches provided Celtic craftsmen with an opportunity to work on a minute scale. (Illustration from Kemble, Franks and Latham, *Horae Ferales*, 1863.)

Blodeuwedd was changed into an owl "and bidden to shun the light of day". According to *The Mabinogion*, the Welsh used the word *"blodeuwedd"* for an owl during the Middle Ages.

CHAPTER VIII

THE ARTHURIAN SAGA

For the majority of modern readers who have not made any special study of the subject, the mention of early British legend will inevitably call up the glories of the Arthurian saga. They will think of the court at Camelot or the fabled palace at Caerleon-on-Usk, the Knights of the Round Table, the Quest of the Grail, the guilty love of Lancelot for the queen, the last great battle by the northern sea, the voyage of Arthur, sorely wounded but immortal, to the mystic valley of Avalon. But as a matter of fact they will find in the native medieval literature of Wales little or nothing of all this, and though there was indeed an Arthur in this literature, he is a wholly different being from the Arthur of what we now call the Arthurian saga.

Tales of a British chief named Arthur were probably taken to Brittany by Welsh exiles at about the sixth century. They must also have brought legends of the Celtic deity Artaius, and these two personages ultimately blended into one. An Arthur saga thus arose, and this became a centre around which clustered a mass of floating legendary matter relating to various Celtic figures, both human and divine. Drawing on these legends, French poets of the twelfth and thirteenth centuries, including Marie de France and Chrestien de Troyes, later wrote the romances which created the basis for the Arthur of the Round Table. Since then, the stories of Arthur and his knights have been adapted and reworked by succeeding generations to become the best-known of all the Celtic legends, and although the versions of Malory and Tennyson are far removed from the *Mabinogion*, they still portray that mixture of wonderful mystery and warlike adventure that is to be found in so many of the most ancient tales.

Into the pantheon of deities represented in the four ancient Welsh *Mabinogi* there came, at a later time, from some other tribal source, another group headed by Arthur, the god Artaius. As the genealogical plan in the previous chapter shows, he takes the place of Gwydion, son of Dôn, and the other deities of his circle fall more or less accurately into the places of others of the earlier circle. His nephews Gwalchmai, Medrawt and Gwalchaved later came to be identified with the knights Gawain, Mordred and Galahad of the French and English romances. Of the tales which follow, that of Kilhwch and Olwen is the only native Arthurian legend which has come down to us in Welsh litera-

Alfred, Lord Tennyson, English poet laureate from 1850 to 1892, reinterpreted the Arthurian myths for a Victorian readership. (Frontispiece to Vol. I of *The Works of Alfred Tennyson*, 1872.)

Kilhwch, the King's Son (opposite), by Arthur Joseph Gaskin (1862–1928). Painted in the style of the Italian Renaissance, Kilhwch appears as a courtly huntsman of the Middle Ages. (Birmingham City Museum and Art Gallery.)

Caerleon-on-Usk, Gwent. This large hollow was thought to be the site of King Arthur's Round Table until archaeological excavation in 1926 revealed the finest Roman amphitheatre in Britain.

A Mounted British Warrior, based on descriptions by Roman authors, is a far cry from the usual picture of Arthur as a knight in shining armour. (From C. Hamilton Smith, *Ancient Costumes of Great Britain and Ireland*, 1814.)

ture. The rest are more or less reflections from the Arthurian literature developed by foreign hands on the Continent.

KILHWCH AND OLWEN

Kilhwch was son to Kilydd and his wife Goleuddydd, and is said to have been cousin to Arthur. His mother having died, Kilydd took another wife, and she, jealous of her stepson, laid on him a quest which promised to be long and dangerous. "I declare," she said, "that it is thy destiny not to be suited with a wife till thou obtain Olwen, daughter of Yspaddaden Penkawr." And Kilhwch reddened at the name, and love of the maiden diffused itself through all his frame. By his father's advice he set out to Arthur's Court to learn how and where he might find and woo her.

After some difficulties with the Porter and with Arthur's seneschal, Kai, who did not wish to admit the lad while the company were sitting at meat, Kilhwch was brought into the presence of the King, and declared his name and his desire.

Arthur, however, had never heard of Olwen nor of her kindred. He promised to seek for her, but at the end of a year, no tidings of her could be found, and Kilhwch declared that he would depart and leave Arthur shamed. Kai and Bedwyr, with the guide Kynddelig, were at last bidden to go forth on the quest.

Kai, it is said, could go nine days under water. He could render himself at will as tall as a forest tree. So hot was his physical constitution that nothing he bore in his hand could get wetted in the heaviest rain. As for Bedwyr, none equalled him in swiftness, and, though one-armed, he was a match for any three warriors on the field of battle; his lance made a wound equal to those of nine. Besides these three there went also on the quest Gwrhyr, who knew all tongues, and Gwalchmai, son of Arthur's sister Gwyar, and Menw, who could make the party invisible by magic spells.

The party journeyed till at last they came to a great castle, before which was a flock of sheep kept by a shepherd who had by him a mastiff big as a horse. The breath of this shepherd could burn up a tree. He let no occasion pass without doing some hurt or harm. However, he received the party well, told them that he was Custennin, brother of Yspaddaden whose castle stood before them, and brought them home to his wife. The wife turned out to be a sister of Kilhwch's mother Goleuddydd, and she rejoiced at seeing her nephew, but was sorrowful at the thought that he had come in search of Olwen, for none ever returned from that quest alive. Custennin and his family had suffered much at the hands of Yspaddaden—all their sons but one being slain, because Yspaddaden envied his brother his share of their patrimony. So they associated themselves with the heroes in their quest.

Next day Olwen came down to the herdsman's house as usual, for she was

The Giant Yspaddaden, father of Olwen, "flung after them a poisoned dart". (Illustration by John D. Batten, for *Celtic Fairy Tales*, edited by Joseph Jacobs, 1892.)

Olwen left her rings in the vessel (left). Decorated with impressed and incised geometric patterns, pottery urns were used throughout Celtic Europe. (Illustration from Kemble, Franks and Latham, *Horae Ferales*, 1863.)

The Tasks of Kilhwch by Dorothea Braby. Only with the help of Arthur's heroes is Kilhwch able to win Olwen for his bride.

Gwrhyr and Eidoel talk with the Eagle of Gwern Abwy, who directs them to the Salmon of Llyn Llyw. (Illustration by John D. Batten for Joseph Jacobs, *Celtic Fairy Tales*, 1892.)

wont to wash her hair there every Saturday, and each time she did so she left all her rings in the vessel and never sent for them again. The maiden was clothed in a robe of flame-coloured silk, and about her neck was a collar of ruddy gold on which were precious emeralds and rubies. Whoever beheld her was filled with her love. Four white trefoils sprang up wherever she trod. And therefore was she called Olwen which means "She of the White Track".

Kilhwch and she conversed together and loved each other, and she bade him go and ask her of her father and deny him nothing that he might demand. She had pledged her faith not to wed without his will, for his life would only last till the time of her espousals.

Next day the party went to the castle and saw Yspaddaden. He put them off with various excuses, and as they left, flung after them a poisoned dart. Bedwyr caught it and flung it back, wounding him in the knee, and Yspaddaden cursed him in language of extraordinary vigour. Thrice over this happened, and at last Yspaddaden declared what must be done to win Olwen.

A vast hill was to be ploughed, sown and reaped in one day; only Amathaon son of Dōn could do it, and he would not. Govannon, the smith, was to rid the ploughshare at each headland, and he would not do it. The two dun oxen of Gwylwyld were to draw the plough, and he would not let them. Honey nine times sweeter than that of the bee had to be got for the wedding feast. A magic cauldron, a magic basket out of which comes any meat that a man desires, a magic horn, the sword of Gwrnach the Giant—all these had to be won; and many other secret and difficult things, some forty in all, before Kilhwch might call Olwen his own. The most difficult quest was that of obtaining the comb and scissors between the two ears of Twrch Trywth, a king transformed into a monstrous boar. To hunt the boar, a number of other quests had first to be accomplished—the whelp of Greid, son of Eri, was to be won, and a certain leash to hold him, and a certain collar for the leash, and a chain for the collar, and Mabon, son of Modron, for the huntsman and the horse of Gweddw to carry Mabon, and so forth, to an extent which makes the famous fire of the sons of Turenn seem trifling by comparison. Kilhwch had one answer for every demand: "It will be easy for me to accomplish this, although thou mayest think that it will not be easy. And I shall gain thy daughter and thou shalt lose thy life."

So they departed on their way to fulfil the tasks, and on their way home they fell in with Gwrnach the Giant, whose sword Kai, pretending to be a sword-polisher, obtained by a strategem. On reaching Arthur's Court again, and telling the King what they had to do, he promised his aid. The first of the marvels they accomplished was the discovery and liberation of Mabon, son of Modron, who was taken from his mother when three nights old. Gwrhyr inquired of him from the Ousel of Cilgwri, who was so old that a smith's anvil on which he was wont to peck had been worn to the size of a nut, yet he had never heard of Mabon. But he took them to a beast older still, the Stag of Redynvre, and so on to the Owl of Cwm Cawlwyd, and the Eagle of Gwern Abwy, and the Salmon of Llyn Llyw, the oldest of living things, and at last they found Mabon imprisoned in the stone dungeon of Gloucester, and with Arthur's help they released him, and so the second task was fulfilled. In one way or another, by strategm, or valour or magic art, every achievement was accomplished, including the last and more perilous one, that of obtaining the blood of the black witch Orddu, daughter of the white witch Orwen, of Penn

Nart Govid on the confines of Hell. Arthur at last cut the hag in two by throwing his knife at her, and Kaw of North Britain took her blood.

So then they set forth for the castle of Yspaddaden again, and he acknowledged defeat. Goreu, son of Custennin, cut off his head, and that night Olwen became the happy bridge of Kilhwch, and the hosts of Arthur dispersed, every man to his own land.

THE DREAM OF RHONABWY

Rhonabwy was a man-at-arms under Madawc, son of Maredudd, whose brother Iorwerth rose in rebellion against him, and Rhonabwy went with the troops of Madawc to put him down. Going with a few companions into a hut to rest for the night, he lay down to sleep on a yellow calf-skin by the fire, while his friends lay on filthy couches of straw and twigs. On the calf-skin he had a wonderful dream. He saw before him the court and camp of Arthur as

King Arthur's great battle with the heathen formed part of the dream of Rhonabwy. (Illustration showing Arthur in combat from a fourteenth-century manuscript in the Bibliothèque Nationale, Paris.)

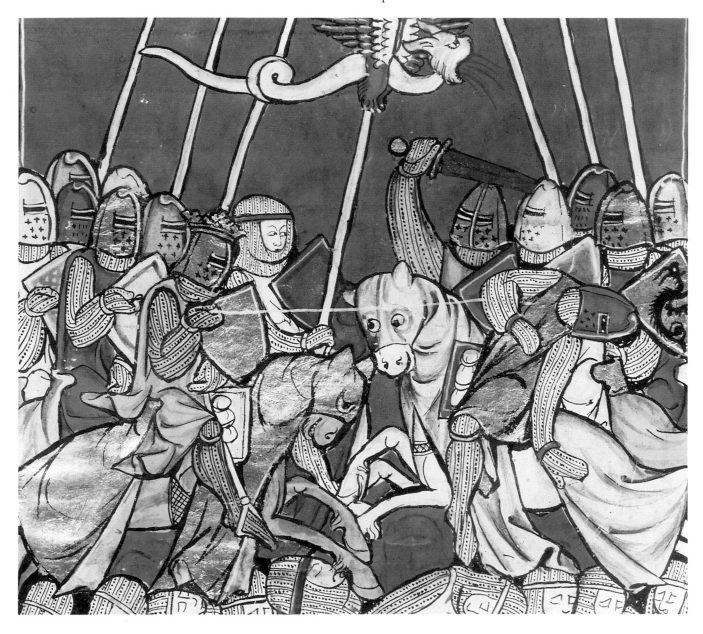

South Cadbury Castle, Somerset, has long been identified with the Arthurian Camelot. The nearby Badbury Rings may be the site of the battle of Mount Badon.

Queen Guinevere (opposite), by William Morris (1834–96). According to one version of the legend, the original Gwenhwyvar, wife of Arthur, came from Cornwall. Her name meant "White Shadow". (Tate Gallery, London.)

he moved towards Mount Badon for his great battle with the heathen. A character named Iddawc was his guide to the King, who smiled at Rhonabwy and his friends, and asked: "Where, Iddawc, did you find these little men?" "I found them, lord, up yonder on the road." "It saddens me," said Arthur, "that men of such stature as these should have the island in their keeping, after the men that guarded it of yore." Rhonabwy had his attention directed to a stone in the King's ring. "It is one of the properties of that stone to enable you to remember that which you see here to-night, and had you not seen the stone, you would never have been able to remember anything of it."

Among those scenes which Rhonabwy witnessed was a game of chess between Arthur and the knight Owain, son of Urien. While the game was going on, first the knights of Arthur harried and disturbed the Ravens of Owain, but Arthur, when Owain complained, only said: "Play your game." Afterwards the Ravens had the better of it, and it was Owain's turn to bid Arthur attend to his game. Then Arthur took the golden chessmen and crushed them to dust in his hand, and besought Owain to quiet his Ravens, which was done, and peace reigned again. Rhonabwy, it is said, slept three days and night on the calf-skin before awaking from his wondrous dream.

THE LADY OF THE FOUNTAIN

We have here a Welsh reproduction of the *Conte* entitled "Le Chevalier au lion" of Chrestien de Troyes. The principal personage in the tale is Owain, son of Urien, who appears in a character as foreign to the spirit of Celtic legend as it was familiar on the Continent, that of knight-errant. However, many details belong to an earlier tradition, among them the magic fountain and silver bowl, and the Black Knight who clearly comes from the otherworld. Indeed, apart from Caerleon, the whole tale appears to take place in a fairy world.

Kymon, a knight of Arthur's Court, had a strange and unfortunate adventure. Riding forth in search of some deed of chivalry to do, he came to a splendid castle, where he was hospitably received by four-and-twenty damsels, of

whom the least lovely was more lovely than Gwenhwyvar, the wife of Arthur. With them was a noble lord, who asked his business. Kymon explained that he was seeking for his match in combat. The lord of the castle smiled, and bade him take the road up the valley and through a forest till he came to a glade with a mound in the midst of it. On the mound he would see a black man of huge stature with one foot and one eye, bearing a mighty iron club. He was wood-ward of that forest, and would have thousands of wild animals feeding around him. He would show Kymon what he was in quest of.

Kymon followed the instructions, and the black man directed him to where he should find a fountain under a great tree; by the side of it would be a silver bowl on a slab of marble. Kymon was to take the bowl and throw a bowlful of water on the slab, when a terrific storm of hail and thunder would follow—then there would break forth an enchanting music of singing birds—then would appear a knight in black armour riding on a coal-black horse, with a black pennon upon his lance.

Kymon did as he was bidden, the Black Knight appeared, silently they set lance in rest and charged. Kymon was flung to earth, while his enemy, not bestowing one glance upon him, passed the shaft of his lance through the rein of Kymon's horse and rode off with it in the direction whence he had come. Kymon went back afoot to the castle, where none asked him how he had sped, but they gave him a new horse on which he rode home to Caerleon.

Owain was fired by the tale of Kymon, and next morning at dawn he rode forth to seek for the same adventure. All passed as it had done in Kymon's case, but Owain wounded the Black Knight so sorely that he turned his horse and fled, Owain pursuing him hotly. They came to a vast and resplendent castle. Across the drawbridge they rode, the outer portcullis of which fell as the Black Knight passed it. But so close at his heels was Owain that the portcullis fell behind him, cutting his horse in two behind the saddle, and he himself remained imprisoned between the outer gate of the drawbridge and the inner. While he was in this predicament, a maiden came to him and gave him a ring. When he wore it with the stone reversed and clenched in his hand he would become invisible, and when the servants of the lord of the castle came for him he was to elude them and follow her.

Owain did as he was bidden, and the maiden concealed him. In that night, a great lamentation was heard in the castle—its lord had died of the wound which Owain had given him. Soon afterwards Owain got sight of the mistress of the castle, and love of her took entire possession of him. Luned, the maiden who had rescued him, wooed her for him, and he became her husband, and

A great serpent. The magical animals of early Celtic myth survived in the more courtly medieval versions of the stories. (Illustration from Standish O'Grady, *Finn and his Companions*, 1892.)

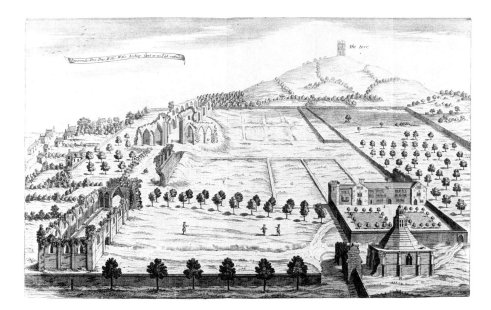

Prospect of Glasenbury Abbey (William Stukeley, *Itinerarium Curiosum*, 1724). According to legend the first church on this site was built by Joseph of Arimathea, who brought the Holy Grail to Britain.

Glactonbury Tor, which overlooks the abbey, is the site of a much earlier tradition, which placed an entrance to Annwn, the Celtic underworld, on this mound.

lord of the Castle of the Fountain and all the dominions of the Black Knight. And he then defended the fountain with lance and sword against all comers as his forerunner had done, and thus he abode for three years.

After this time Arthur, with his nephew Gwalchmai and with Kymon for guide, rode forth at the head of a host to search for tidings of Owain. They came to the fountain, and here they met Owain, neither knowing the other as their helms were down. And first Kai was overthrown, and then Gwalchmai and Owain fought, and after a while Gwalchmai was unhelmed. Owain said, "My lord Gwalchmai, I did not know you; take my sword and my arms." Said Gwalchmai, "You Owain, are the victor; take my sword." Arthur ended the contention in courtesy by taking the swords of both, and then they all rode to the Castle of the Fountain, where Owain entertained them with great joy. And he went back with Arthur to Caerleon, promising to his countess that he would remain there but three months and then return.

But at the Court of Arthur he forgot his love and his duty, and remained there three years. At the end of that time, a noble lady came riding upon a horse caparisoned with gold, and she sought out Owain and took the ring from his hand. "Thus", she said, "shall be treated the deceiver, the traitor, the faithless, the disgraced and the beardless." Then she turned her horse's head and departed. And Owain, overwhelmed with shame and remorse, fled from the sight of men and lived in a desolate country with wild beasts.

When near to death from exposure and want, he was taken in by a certain widowed countess and her maidens, and restored to strength by magic balsams, and although they besought him to remain with them, he rode forth again, seeking for lonely and desert lands. Here he found a lion in battle with a great serpent. Owain slew the serpent, and the lion followed him and played about him as if it had been a greyhound that he had reared. And it fed him by catching deer, part of which Owain cooked for himself, giving the rest to his lion to devour, and the beast kept watch over him by night.

Owain next found an imprisoned damsel, whose sights he heard, though he could not see her nor she him. Being questioned, she told him that her name was Luned—she was the handmaid of a countess whose husband had left her. Two of the pages of the countess had traduced him, and because she defended him she was condemned to be burned if before a year was out he (namely, Owain, son of Urien) had not appeared to deliver her. And the year would end

Fortifications of the Brigantes at Stanwick, N. Yorks. Evrawc, the name of Peredur's father, is derived from Eburacum, the Roman name for York.

tomorrow. On the next day Owain rescued Luned, and returned to the Castle of the Fountain, where he was reconciled with his love. And he took her with him to Arthur's Court, and she was his wife there as long as she lived.

THE TALE OF PEREDUR

The Tale of Peredur is one of great interest and significance in connexion with the origin of the Grail legend. Peredur corresponds to the Perceval of Chrestien de Troyes, to whom we owe the earliest extant poem on the Grail; but that writer left his Grail story unfinished, and we never learn from him what exactly the Grail was or what gave it its importance. When we turn for light to "Peredur," which undoubtedly represents a more ancient form of the legend, we find ourselves baffled. For "Peredur" may be described as the Grail story without the Grail.

Peredur was a seventh son, which was equivalent to being marked out by destiny for fortunes high and strange. His father, Evrawc, an earl of the North, and his six brothers had fallen in fight. Peredur's mother, therefore, fearing a similar fate for her youngest child, brought him up in a forest, keeping from him all knowledge of chivalry or warfare. Here he grew up a simple rustic in manner and in knowledge, but of an amazing bodily strength and activity.

One day he saw three knights on the borders of the forest. They were all of Arthur's Court—Gwalchmai, Geneir and Owain. Entranced by the sight, he asked his mother what these beings were. "They are angels, my son," said she.

"By my faith", said Peredur, "I will go and become an angel with them." He went to meet them, and soon learned what they were. That evening he picked out a bony piebald draught-horse, and dressed him up in a saddle and trapping made of twigs, and imitated from those he had seen. Seeing that he was bent on going, his mother gave him her blessing and sundry instructions, and bade him seek the Court of Arthur, where there were the best, and the boldest, and the most beautiful of men.

Peredur mounted his horse, took for weapons a handful of sharp-pointed stakes, and rode forth to Arthur's Court. Here the steward, Kai, rudely repulsed him for his rustic appearance, but a dwarf and dwarfess, who had been a year at the Court without speaking one word to any one there, cried: "Goodly Peredur, son of Evrawc, the welcome of Heaven be unto you, flower of knights and light of chivalry." Kai chastised the dwarfs for breaking silence by lauding such a fellow as Peredur, and when the latter demanded to be brought to Arthur, bade him first go and overcome a stranger knight who had just challenged the whole Court by throwing a goblet of wine into the face of Gwenhwyvar, and whom all shrank from meeting. Peredur went out promptly to where the ruffian knight was swaggering up and down, pierced his skull with one of his sharp stakes and slew him. Owain then came out and found Peredur dragging his fallen enemy about. "What are you doing there?" said Owain. "This iron coat", said Peredur, "will never come off from him; not by my efforts, at any rate." So Owain showed him how to unfasten the armour, and Peredur took it, and the knight's weapons and horse, and rode forth to seek what further adventures might befall.

Peredur, on leaving Arthur's Court, had many encounters in which he triumphed with ease, sending the beaten knights to Caerleon-on-Usk with the message that he had overthrown them for the honour of Arthur and in his service, but that he, Peredur, would never come to the Court again till he had avenged the insult to the dwarfs upon Kai, who was accordingly reproved by Arthur and was greatly grieved thereat.

Peredur came to a castle beside a lake, where he found a venerable man with attendants about him who were fishing in the lake. As Peredur approached, the aged man rose and went into the castle, and Peredur saw that he was lame. Peredur entered, and was hospitably received in a great hall. The aged man asked him, when they had done their meal, if he knew how to fight with the sword, and promised to teach him all knightly accomplishments, adding "I am your uncle, your mother's brother." Finally, he bade him ride forth, and remember, whatever he saw that might cause him wonder, not to ask the meaning of it if no one had the courtesy to inform him.

On next riding forth, Peredur came to a vast desert wood, beyond which he found a great castle, the Castle of Wonders. He entered it by the open door, and found a stately, hoary-headed man sitting in a great hall with many pages about him, who received Peredur honourably. At meat Peredur sat beside the lord of the castle, who asked him, when they had done, if he could fight with a sword. "Were I to receive instruction", said Peredur, "I think I could." The lord then gave Peredur a sword, and bade him strike at a great iron staple that was in the floor. Peredur did so, and cut the staple in two, but the sword also flew into two parts. "Place the two parts together," said the lord. Peredur did so, and they became one again. A second time this was done with the same result. The third time neither sword nor staple would reunite.

Peredur's rustic appearance provoked the mockery of Arthur's steward Kai. (Illustration from C. Hamilton Smith, *Ancient Costumes of Great Britain and Ireland*, 1814.)

A strange knight threw a goblet of wine into the face of Gwenhwyvar. Bronze flagon with coral and enamel inlay from Basse Vutz, Lorraine, fourth century B.C. (British Museum).

"You have arrived," said the lord, "at two-thirds of your strength." He then declared that he also was Peredur's uncle, and brother to the fisher-lord with whom Peredur had lodged on the previous night. As they discoursed, two youths entered the hall bearing a spear of mighty size, from the point of which three streams of blood dropped upon the ground, and all the company when they saw this began wailing and lamenting, but the lord took no notice and did not break off his discourse with Peredur. Next there came in two maidens carrying between them a large salver, on which, amid a profusion of blood, lay a man's head. Thereupon the wailing and lamenting began even more loudly than before. But at last they fell silent, and Peredur was led off to his chamber. Mindful of the injunction of the fisher-lord, he had shown no surprise at what he saw, nor had he asked the meaning of it. He then rode forth again in quest of other adventures. Finally it was revealed that the head in the silver dish was that of a cousin of Peredur's. The lance was the weapon with which he was slain, and with which also the uncle of Peredur, the fisher-lord, had been lamed. Peredur had been shown these things to incite him to avenge the wrong, and to prove his fitness for the task. The nine sorceresses of Gloucester worked these evils on the relatives of Peredur. On learning these matters Peredur, with the help of Arthur, attacked the sorceresses, who were slain, every one, and the vengeance was accomplished.

Detail from *Quest for the Holy Grail*. A tapestry woven by William Morris & Co., after Edward Burne-Jones. The original tale of Peredur, which was wholly pagan, gave rise to many Christian reinterpretations. (The Birmingham City Museum and Art Gallery.)

THE TALE OF TALIESIN

There lived, it was said, in the time of Arthur, a man named Tegid Voel of Penllyn, whose wife was named Ceridwen. They had a son named Avagddu, who was the most ill-favoured man in the world. To compensate for his lack of beauty, his mother resolved to make him a sage. So she began to boil a cauldron of inspiration and science for her son. The cauldron might not cease to boil for a year and a day, and only in three drops of it were to be found the magical grace of the brew. She put Gwion Bach, the son of Gwreang of

Ceridwen became a greyhound and pursued Gwion Bach, disguised as a hare. Hare and greyhound, from the Book of Kells (Trinity College, Dublin).

Ceridwen then became a black hen so that she could swallow Gwion Bach, who had turned himself into a grain of wheat. Hen from the Book of Kells (Trinity College, Dublin).

Llanfair, to stir the cauldron, and a blind man named Morda to keep the fire going, and she made incantations over it and put in magical herbs from time to time. But one day towards the end of the year, three drops of the magic liquor flew out of the cauldron and lighted on the finger of Gwion. He put his finger in his mouth, and immediately became gifted with supernatural insight. He saw that he had got what was intended for Avagddu, and he saw that Ceridwen would destroy him for it if she could. So he fled to his own land.

Ceridwen now came on the scene and saw that her year's labour was lost. In her rage she smote Morda with a billet of firewood and struck out his eye, and she then pursued Gwion Bach. He saw her and changed himself into a hare. She became a greyhound. He leaped into a river and became a fish, and she chased him as an otter. He became a bird and she a hawk. Then he turned himself into a grain of wheat and dropped among the other grains on a threshing-floor, and she became a black hen and swallowed him. Nine months afterwards she bore him as an infant, and she would have killed him, but could not on account of his beauty, so she wrapped him in a leather bag, and cast him into the sea to the mercy of God.

Now Gwyddno had a salmon weir on the strand between Dyvi and Aberystwyth. And his son Elphin one day fished out the leather bag as it stuck on the weir. They opened it, and found the infant within. "Taliesin be he called," said Elphin. And they brought the child home very carefully and reared it as their own. And this was Taliesin, prime bard of the Cymry, and the first of the poems he made was a lay of praise to Elphin and promise of good fortune for the future. And this was fulfilled, for Elphin grew in riches and honour day after day, and in love and favour with King Arthur.

But one day as men praised King Arthur and all his belongings above measure, Elphin boasted that he had a wife as virtuous as any at Arthur's Court and a bard more skilful than any of the King's, and they flung him into prison until they should see if he could make good his boast. And as he lay there with a silver chain about his feet, a graceless fellow named Rhun was sent to court the wife of Elphin and to bring back proof of her folly.

Taliesin then bade his mistress conceal herself, and she gave her raiment and jewels to one of the kitchen-maids, who received Rhun as if she were mistress of the household. And after supper, Rhun plied the maid with drink, and she became intoxicated and fell in a deep sleep, whereupon Rhun cut off one of her fingers, on which was the signet-ring of Elphin that he had sent his wife a little while before. Rhun brought the finger and the ring on it to Arthur's Court.

Next day Elphin was fetched out of prison and shown the finger and the ring. Whereupon he said: "With your leave, mighty king, I cannot deny the ring, but the finger it is on was never my wife's. For this is the little finger, and the ring fits tightly on it, but my wife could barely keep it on her thumb. And my wife, moreover, is wont to pare her nails every Saturday night, but this nail hath not been pared for a month. And thirdly, the hand to which this finger belonged was kneading rye-dough within three days past, but my wife has never kneaded rye-dough since my wife she has been."

Then the King was angry because his test had failed, and he ordered Elphin back to prison till he could prove what he had affirmed about his bard. Then Taliesin went to court, and one high day when the Kings' bards and minstrels should sing and play before him, Taliesin, as they passed him sitting quietly in a corner, pouted his lips and played "Blerwm, blerwm" with his finger on his mouth. And when the bards came to perform before the King, lo! a spell was

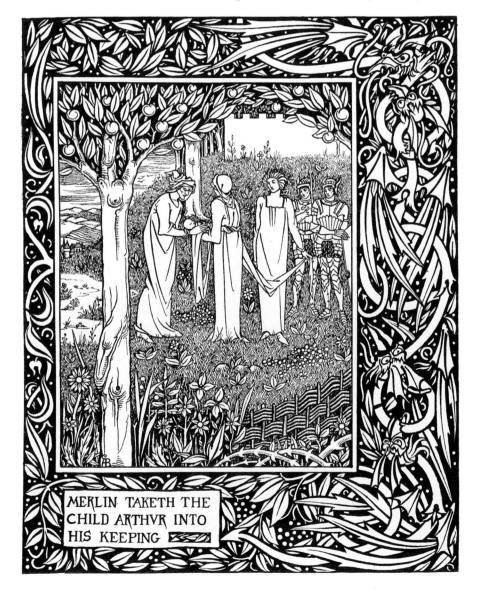

MERLIN TAKETH THE CHILD ARTHVR INTO HIS KEEPING

Merlin taketh the child Arthur into his keeping. The wizard Merlin was partly based on the bard Myrddin, a contemporary of Taliesin. (Illustration by Aubrey Beardsley for Thomas Malory's *Morte d'Arthur.*)

Secret things of the past were identified by Celtic legends with such prehistoric monuments as the Castlerigg stone circle in the Lake District, home of the bard Myrddin.

on them, and they could do nothing but bow before him and play "Blerwm, blerwm" with their fingers on their lips. And the chief of them, Heinin, said: "O king, we be not drunken with wine, but are dumb through the influence of the spirit that sits in yon corner under the form of a child." Then Taliesin was brought forth, and they asked him who he was and whence he came. And he sang his story to them.

While Taliesin sang a great storm of wind arose, and the castle shook with the force of it. Then the King bade Elphin be brought in before him, and when he came, at the music of Taliesin's voice and harp the chains fell open of themselves and he was free. And many other poems concerning secret things of the past and future did Taliesin sing before the King and his lords, and he foretold the coming of the Saxon into the land, and his oppression of the Cymry, and foretold also his passing away when the day of his destiny should come.

THE STORY OF TRISTAN AND ISOLDE

One of the best known of the Arthurian legends was first written down in Anglo-Norman French, although its Celtic origins are indisputable. Its connections with Arthur's court are somewhat tenuous, and were probably added by the medieval romance writers who hoped to exploit the popularity of the Arthurian saga.

An orphan, young Tristan was sent to the court of his uncle, King Mark of Cornwall, at Tintagel. Three years later the day of reckoning came for the tribute which Mark owed to the Morholt, brother of the Queen of Ireland. Tristan resolved to fight the Morholt and, although he himself was wounded by the other's poisoned sword he succeeded in killing him, but he left a fragment of his sword in the Morholt's head.

On returning to Cornwall he was welcomed by the King, but his wound became worse and he decided to take to the sea, leaving his voyage to chance as to whether he found death or cure. He landed in Ireland and there he was nursed back to health by the Queen and her daughter Isolde, from whom he concealed his real name, calling himself Tantris.

When Tristan came back to Cornwall, Mark offered to make him heir to the throne, for he had no children. But his barons were jealous and insisted that the King marry. To appease them he said he would marry only the girl whose golden hair had just been brought him by a swallow. Tristan recognized the hair as Isolde's and offered to go and ask for her hand on Mark's behalf.

When he arrived in Ireland, disguised as a merchant, the country was being terrorized by a fierce dragon. Tristan succeeded in killing the beast, but contact with its poisonous tongue rendered him unconscious and an imposter claimed the victory, and with it the hand of Isolde which the Irish king had offered as a reward. Suspecting trickery, Isolde and the Queen found Tristan and again

Tristram and Isoud setting sail for Cornwall, where Isoud was to marry King Mark. (Illustration from medieval manuscript in the Bibliothèque Nationale, Paris.)

Tintagel. This spectacular site contains the remains of both a medieval castle and a Celtic monastery. Apart from its connections with the Tristan legend, it is also said to be the birthplace of King Arthur.

How Sir Tristram drank of the love drink, a magic potion intended for Isolde and Mark on their wedding night. (Illustration by Aubrey Beardsley for Thomas Malory's *Morte d'Arthur*.)

nursed him back to health. But while doing so, they found his sword and saw that a piece missing from it matched the fragment in the Morholt's body. Isolde threatened to avenge her uncle's death, but finally yielded to Tristan's persuasions. As true slayer of the monster he would become her husband. Tristan said that he had come to ask for Isolde for his uncle Mark and the King agreed.

Before they left Ireland the Queen secretly gave Isolde's maid Brangwain a philtre containing a magic potion which ensured undying love between those who drank it. This was to be given to Isolde and Mark on their wedding night. However, on the boat returning to Cornwall, Tristan and Isolde accidentally drank the potion and immediately felt an irrestistible love for each other. But Isolde was promised to Mark and had to marry him.

Despite his feelings of loyalty towards his uncle, Tristan could not prevent himself from loving Isolde, nor she him. They continued to meet, their favourite place being an orchard. The barons warned the King, who decided to surprise the lovers by lying in wait for them in a pine-tree in the middle of the orchard. But they noticed his reflection in a fountain and avoided the trap.

Eventually King Mark did find them together, and furious at his nephew's betrayal, he condemned Tristan to death and banished Isolde to live among a band of lepers. Tristan escaped, rescued Isolde and the two lovers fled to the Forest of Morois. There one day Mark found them sleeping with Tristan's sword between them. He could not bring himself to kill them but instead exchanged his own sword for Tristan's. When they awoke, the lovers recognized that Mark had shown them mercy and, determined to make their peace with him, they returned to court.

To decide the matter, Mark asked for the judgment of King Arthur, who declared that Isolde should remain with each man for half the year. Mark chose the season when there were no leaves on the trees, to which Isolde joyfully responded that then she would belong always to Tristan since the holly, ivy and crypress keep their leaves all year.

Finally unable to bear the situation any longer, Tristan left Cornwall and went to Brittany. There he married a Breton princess, Isolde of the White Hands, but their marriage was never consummated because Tristan could not

HOW SIR TRISTRAM DRANK OF THE LOVE DRINK

forget his first love. Kaherdin, his new wife's brother, learned his secret, and when Tristan was wounded in an expedition, it was Kaherdin he sent to Cornwall to bring back Queen Isolde.

The arrangement was that if Kaherdin was successful, he was to put a white sail on his boat; if he failed, a black sail, so that Tristan would be able to see from the shore whether the Queen had come to him. Too ill to watch himself, Tristan asked his wife to tell him when Kaherdin's boat was approaching. And she, being consumed with jealousy, told him that a white sail was black. Lacking the strength to continue living, Tristan died. Finding her lover dead, Isolde also died, and the lovers were buried side by side.

LANCELOT, OR THE KNIGHT OF THE CART

This account, based on the tale by Chrestien de Troyes, is full of those touches of courtly romance which came to overlay the original Celtic legends. Nevertheless, elements of Celtic mystery and magic remain, and the story provides an interesting bridge between the Arthur of Welsh literature and the Arthur of later French and English writers, who set their hero against the background of the Middle Ages and medieval notions of chivalry.

King Arthur was holding court at Camelot when an unknown knight appeared. He said that he had taken several of Arthur's knights prisoner and demanded that Queen Guinevere be given to him as a hostage. To obtain their release Arthur was to send a champion into the forest to do battle with him. Sir Kay, the king's seneschal, took up the challenge and rode out to meet the unknown knight. But in a little while his horse returned without its rider.

The king's nephew, Gavain, then departed in search of the Queen. On his way he came across another unknown knight whose horse was about to give way beneath him. To this man Gavain gave one of his horses, but a little while later he found the dead body of the horse he had given surrounded by broken weapons. It appeared that some violent combat had taken place. A little further along the road he saw the knight, in full armour, following a cart driven by a dwarf. It was the kind of cart used to carry criminals through the town to their punishment. The knight asked the dwarf if he had seen the Queen, and the

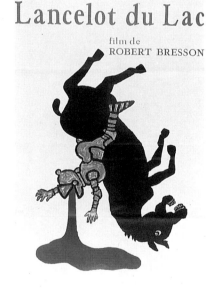

Lancelot du Lac, poster for film directed by Robert Bresson (1974), in which the relationship between Guinevere and Lancelot forms the central theme.

Bronze harness mounts from South Shields, late second century. It was a measure of Lancelot's love for Guinevere that he agreed to ride in a cart. An honourable knight ought to have remained mounted on his horse. (Museum of Antiquities, Newcastle-upon-Tyne.)

dwarf told him that if he would know what had happened to her, he must ride in the cart. After hesitating for a while, he decided he must sacrifice his honour for the sake of the Queen, whom he loved, and mounted the cart.

Paying no heed to the jeers and questions of any people they passed, the knight allowed himself to be driven in the cart to a grand castle, with Gavain following him to see what should become of him. That night, from the castle window, the knight saw Meleagant, son of King Bademagu, taking Queen Guinevere to the land of Gorre, whence no stranger returned. Gavain and the knight of the cart set out to rescue her. There were two paths into the land of Gorre: one by the Bridge under the water, which Gavain took, and one by the Bridge of the Sword, which was chosen by the unknown knight as being more direct.

This terrible bridge consisted of a blade, guarded, apparently, by two lions on the far side. Paying no heed to the warnings of his companions the knight crawled laboriously along the sword, cutting himself fearfully on his hands and feet as he went. And when he finally reached the far side, he remembered the lions, but could find no sign of them. Then he realized that he had been deceived by a spell.

When he had recovered, the knight engaged in a terrible combat with Meleagant. It seemed that Meleagant might carry the day when Guinevere's maid, who was watching from a nearby window with the Queen herself, hit upon a trick to encourage him. "Who is that knight?" she asked, and the Queen replied, "His name is Lancelot du Lac." Then the maid called him by name and told him to turn and see the Queen. With the sight of Guinevere, whom he loved, Lancelot found new strength and overcame his opponent. At the Queen's request he spared his defeated enemy, but he could not win her favour because he had hesitated before climbing onto the cart and it was Gavain who had the honour of returning Guinevere to the king.

Lancelot in the Cart. Paying no heed to the jeers and questions of the people around him, Lancelot mounts the cart for the sake of the Queen. (Illustration from medieval manuscript in the Bibliothèque Nationale.)

INDEX

INDEX

ACKNOWLEDGEMENTS

James Austin, Cambridge: 14 (right); Bibliothèque Nationale, Paris: 133, 137; Birmingham City Museums and Art Gallery: 120; Janet and Colin Bord, Corwen, Clwyd: 13, 21 (bottom), 47 (with Anthony Weir), 89 (top) (with Anthony Weir), 96, 103, 111, 113 (bottom), 122 (right), 126, 129, 136, 138; The Bridgeman Art Library, London: 15, 26 (bottom), 43, 51, 62, 100, 104, 125, 127, 132, 133; British Film Institute, London: 14 (left), 140 (left); British Museum, London (by courtesy of the Trustees): half-title page, 44, 46, 53, 64, 67, 69, 72, 86 (left), 94, 109 (bottom), 135, 140 (right); J Allan Cash, London: opposite title page, 10, 81, 84; J-L Charmet, Paris: 11 (left); City of Dundee District Council: 36; E T Archive, London: 87, 114; Sonia Halliday, Weston Turville, Bucks: 88 (left); Irish Tourist Board, Dublin: 11 (right), 29 (bottom), 37 (top), 41, 49 (bottom), 56 (top), 82, 83; Billie Love, Ryde, Isle of Wight: 19 (right), 28; Magnum, London: 58 (top), 67, 71, 102, 118; MPL, Bath: IV, 7 (top), 19 (left), 26 (top), 33, 36 (top), 39, 49 (top), 61, 68, 76, 86, 90, 105, 115 (bottom), 119 (top), 121, 123 (left), 135, 139; National Museum of Denmark, Copenhagen: 48, 87, 112; National Museum of Ireland, Dublin: 58 (bottom); Northern Irish Tourist Board, Belfast: 52; Eddie Ryle Hodges, Co. Durham: 9, 130; Ronald Sheridan, London: 23, 73 (left), 88 (left), 106; Edwin Smith Archive, Saffron Walden: 20 (bottom), 21 (top), 22, 25 (left), 27, 29 (top), 37 (bottom), 42, 45, 59, 65, 75, 80 (right), 88 (right), 110, 113 (top); Society of Antiquaries, London: 16; Somerset County Museums Service: 8; Welsh Folk Museum, Cardiff: 20 (top).

PUBLISHER'S NOTE: The publishers have made every effort to locate and credit the copyright holders of material reproduced in this book, and they regret any errors or omissions that may have occurred.